Forensic Analysis and DNA in Criminal Investigations: Including Cold Cases Solved

by RJ Parker
and Peter Vronsky (Preface)

Forensic Analysis and DNA in Criminal Investigations: Including Cold Cases Solved

by RJ Parker
and Peter Vronsky (Preface)

Copyrights and Published by

RJ Parker Publishing, Inc.
http://m.RJPARKERPUBLISHING.com

ISBN-13: 978-1514348369
ISBN-10: 1514348365

Printed in the United States of America
(10.2015)

Copyright

Acknowledgements

Thank you to the following individuals for your encouragement and help in preparing this book:

Marlene Fabregas
Darlene Horn
Kim Jackson
Robyn MacEachern
Katherine McCarthy
Bettye McKee
Ron Steed

Contents

Preface:

The Pioneering Days, a Brief History
By Peter Vronsky

Humanoids have been around for a million years—our species of homo-sapiens for about a hundred thousand—we came out of the cave and bush and became "civilized" about fifteen thousand years ago, and until about only two hundred years ago, we were a very chaotic and disorganized species, so disorganized that there did not even exist such a thing as a police department, let alone forensic science. Order was kept by standing military forces, who mainly were concerned with keeping the "King's peace," thus the European term *gendarme*—or "men at arms." In the English-speaking world, the term "constable" had its origins in an ancient Byzantine era term: *comes stabuli*, meaning "master of the stable." English King's commanders of mounted knight enforcers came to be known as constables until the term was modernized and bureaucratized in the modern age. The term "police" meant to implement "policy" and there was no such thing as a municipal police department in the English-speaking world until the founding of the London Metropolitan Police in 1829, which only relatively recently ushered into the world our modern concept of a police department as we now know it. And even then, for the first fifty years police mostly "prevented" crime by patrolling on the beat and ensuring people and property were secure. They did not do much investigating once a crime was perpetrated and the reason why is simple: forensic sciences and investigative techniques had not yet caught up to the nineteenth-century scientific world in which the seeds of modern policing and law enforcement were being first planted. Policing was emerging in a rapidly changing age of sciences and the merging of the two was spectacular when it began to unfold.

Since Dr. Edmond Locard (13 December 1877 – 4 May 1966), a pioneer in forensic science who became known as the Sherlock Holmes of France, first formulated the basic principle of forensic science: "Every contact leaves a trace," also known as "Locard's Exchange Principle." While police authorities struggled to bring the sciences into criminal investigations, Locard argued that the perpetrator of a crime will bring something into the crime scene and leave with something from it, and that both can be used as forensic evidence. He stated:

> Wherever he steps, whatever he touches, whatever he leaves, even unconsciously, will serve as a silent witness against him. Not only his fingerprints or his footprints, but his hair, the fibers

from his clothes, the glass he breaks, the tool mark he leaves, the paint he scratches, the blood or semen he deposits or collects. All of these and more, bear mute witness against him. This is evidence that does not forget. It is not confused by the excitement of the moment. It is not absent because human witnesses are. It is factual evidence. Physical evidence cannot be wrong, it cannot perjure itself, it cannot be wholly absent. Only human failure to find it, study and understand it, can diminish its value.

One of the first fields to attempt to define a systematic scientific approach to forensic investigative techniques was that of physical identification experts, who gathered in 1885, in Rome, at the first International Congress for Criminal Anthropology. According to an observer from the Smithsonian Institution, the conference "opened a new epoch in the history of crime... It was proposed to investigate crime scientifically, biologically, fundamentally; to investigate its origins, its causes."[1]

Led by Italian criminologist Ceasare Lombroso in a post-Darwinian age of natural selection and genetic

[1] Starr, Douglas (2010-10-05). The Killer of Little Shepherds: A True Crime Story and the Birth of Forensic Science (Kindle Locations 2498-2500). Knopf Doubleday Publishing Group. Kindle Edition.

predisposition, the criminal anthropologists believed that criminals could be identified *before* they committed a crime (like in the futuristic Tom Cruise movie *Minority Report*) because they were genetically and physically predisposed to be criminals. In other words, people were born criminal, according to this school of criminology, and therefore criminals had certain distinguishing physical characteristics by which they could be identified as criminally predisposed even before they committed their first crime. But it was in the end proven to be 'quack science' and came crashing down a decade later when social and environmental factors were identified by the broader forensic sciences community as the leading causes of criminal behavior, not genetic predisposition alone.

Gradually forensic sciences began to develop simultaneously in several different fields: the identification of the criminal offender; the identification of the victim; the identification of the means and time of death; the discovery of evidence invisible to the human eye, the ability to collect and preserve it and systematically catalogue and classify that evidence from fingerprints and barrel grooves on a bullet to blood types and DNA trace evidence today. The complexity and breadth of different forensic sciences as they developed over the last 150 years is breathtaking, as were the various rise and falls of what was thought to be various forensic sciences that were exposed as not as 'scientific' as first thought, as for example, Lombroso's theory of the physically identifiable "criminal type." But even so, Lombroso's focus on the physical characteristics of criminals led to France's Alphonse Bertillon to introduce a system of identification based on a series of physical characteristics that would be measured and carefully entered into a criminal's file. It was thought that no two people could have a similar combination of characteristics. The process became known as the Bertillon anthropometric identification system, and it even included fingerprints, but as in modern police work, the flaw was often not in the system but in the way the data was stored and retrieved. Police departments did not file records by fingerprint type but by Bertillon measurement instead. The entire system came crashing down in 1911 when a workman in the Louvre stole the *Mona Lisa.* The French police had his fingerprints on file but their records were filed by Bertillon measurements and not fingerprint pattern. Had the police used fingerprint data in the filing system they would have been able to quickly identify the perpetrator but instead it took them years. By the first decade of the twentieth century, police departments around the world quickly learned that while Bertillon records might help identify somebody already suspected, fingerprints unlike

Bertillon measurements could be lifted at a crime scene and lead police to an unidentified perpetrator if their records are filed by fingerprint. By the 1910s most police departments began to abandon the Bertillon system in favour of the fingerprint classification system.

One of the earliest and most urgent development of forensic sciences was toxicology—the detection of poisons. While science was constantly introducing new potentially lethal substances if administrated in massive doses that would mimic natural forms of death—morphine (1803); strychnine (1818); brucine (1819; quinine (1820); conium (derived from hemlock; 1826); pure nicotine (1828); chloroform (1831); codeine (1832); and aconite and belladonna (extracted from deadly nightshade; 1833)—there were no chemical tests developed for any of these new potentially deadly substances. The most used poison for murder in that epoch was arsenic, a common ingredient not only in rat poison but in beauty products as well, reputed to cure pimples and blemishes. It was cheap, at ten pennies an ounce in the 1840s and it was colorless, odorless, and soluble in hot water. Two to four grains—a fraction of a teaspoon—was lethal (there are 437.5 grains to an ounce.) The challenge facing forensic experts in arsenic murder cases was not a test to detect arsenic, but a test that would dramatically demonstrate to juries the presence of arsenic. A so-called Scheele test invented back in the eighteenth century revealed the presence of arsenic by releasing a garlic-like smell. But how does one produce a smell before a jury? Juries in those days by their nature were suspicious of "scientific experts" in an age when one "science" after another was being debunked. It was only in 1840 that British chemist James Marsh devised a test that produced a visible indication of arsenic that could be brought persuasively before a jury, where jurors could see it with their own eyes. The so-called Marsh arsenic test became the definitive tool in forensic toxicology to combat an epidemic of arsenic poisoning in mid-nineteenth century Europe.

With the evolution of firearms the science of forensic ballistics began to slowly evolve. The earliest recorded case of ballistic identification in a murder case comes from 1794 in the murder of Edward Culshaw, found shot dead through the head in Prescot, England. The surgeon examining the victim discovered a wad of paper inside the wound, used to pack the ball and charge in the flintlock pistol used as the murder weapon. When the partly burned wad was unfolded, it revealed a fragment from a street ballad. Suspicion had originally fallen on John Toms, an eighteen-year-old youth who was taken into custody. Authorities found in his coat pocket the same printed street ballad with a missing fragment that matched the one extracted from the victim's wound.

An early pioneer in forensic identification and investigation was British detective Henry Goddard, whose investigation of an alleged burglary in 1835 revealed a glimpse into the future of forensics. Goddard was investigating a burglary reported by a butler who reported being awakened in his mistress's house when his bedroom door was opened by a man carrying a bulls-eye lantern that casted, according to the butler, a shadow of the man before it. Behind him was a second man, the butler claimed. As he drew his own pistol, the butler said, one of the men fired a shot toward him, which barely missed him and embedded itself in the bed board behind him. The butler claimed he chased the two masked men into the corridor, where he struggled with them until they escaped, abandoning the loot behind them.

Goddard's suspicions were immediately aroused by the butler's claim that the lantern cast a shadow of a man before it, an illogical assertion. Inspecting the door through which the burglars had allegedly made their entrance, Goddard noticed marks from a crowbar. But when crowbarring a door, marks are left on both sides of a door as the bar is leveraged against the doorframe. Goddard noticed that the marks were not aligned correctly. The forcing of the door had been staged from both sides, as were the marks on the closet door, behind which the valuables were stored.

Goddard seized the butler's pistol and his ammunition and then proceeded to dig out the ball that had been allegedly fired into the bed-board. Goddard found the ball flattened but could see it was of similar size and caliber as the pistol the butler carried. Today of course, bullets are easily matched by the groove marks left on a bullet to the exact weapon from which they were fired, but old world smoothbore flintlock pistols left no grooves. The ammunition might be similar, but how to prove it was the same? But Goddard noticed a tiny pimple on all of the butler's ammo just the same as on the flattened ball from the bed-board. Seizing now the butler's mold in which he poured his lead balls from, Goddard detected a tiny defective hole in the mold that fit the pimple on the ammunition. The butler had staged the entire burglary to trick his mistress in giving him a reward for saving her property.

It was a case in New York State in 1915 that revealed both the challenge and the need of an advanced forensic ballistic analysis system in the United States. Charles Stielow, a farmhand in Orleans County, NY, was accused of shooting his employer and housekeeper in a robbery with a .22-caliber pistol. When it was discovered that Stielow owned a .22 handgun, he was charged and a ballistic "expert" was called in to testify in court. In those days, forensic experts were not certified or accredited; many were self-proclaimed charlatans, and this one testified that there was a perfect match between the bullets recovered from the victims and Stielow's handgun. Stielow was convicted and sent to prison. But he was lucky. The Governor of New York was familiar with the case and personally unconvinced of the guilt of Stielow and launched a second investigation to which an assistant in the New York district attorney's office was assigned: Charles E. Waite—the future father of American ballistic forensic sciences.

Waite determined that the Stielow's pistol had never been fired. The "expert" had made up his testimony. After firing the pistol and comparing the bullets, it became clear that the bullets from the victims did not match the pistol that Stielow owned and he was released from prison. The case, however, made Charles E. Waite obsessed with now cataloguing all the firearms in the United States. Back in England, Robert Churchill had already catalogued 119 .25-caliber weapons there, and so Waite felt it was no obstacle to simple contact every manufacturer making handguns since Colt and Smith and Wesson first began mass producing weapons for public consumption. After three years of work, Waite had catalogued almost every

American-made weapon. Then, to his shock, he discovered that European weapons were also flooding the marketplace in the U.S. He then set off for Europe and added another 1,500 weapons to his catalogued collection.

Waite was also aware of the claim made by Victor Balthazard in 1912 that every weapon leaves its own individual signature like a fingerprint. No two handguns, even of the same model, leave the same marks on a bullet and cartridge. The rifling in the barrel and its imperfections mark a bullet with very particular and unique patterns while a firing pin and extractor also leave unique characteristic marks on the cartridge. A single individual weapon can be identified. But how?

Waite now approached Max Poser an optics expert in the Bausch and Lomb Optical Company in Rochester to construct a custom microscope to inspect bullets. Together with physicist John H. Fischer and chemist Philip O. Gravelle, Waite set up the Bureau of Forensic Ballistics in New York in 1923. Fischer now developed an instrument called the helixometer, a hollow probe with illumination and magnifying optics designed for looking down a gun barrel while Gravelle designed the comparison microscope, still used today to compare two halves of separate bullets together under the same lens as if they were one to detect matches.

Waite died of a heart attack in 1926, but his assistant, an ex-U.S. Army officer, Calvin Goddard, carried on Waite's work in the cataloging of new weapons and advancing the science of ballistic forensics. Goddard arrived on the scene just in time for the Roaring Twenties in Chicago. He was called out in 1929 to Chicago to assist in the investigation of the mass gangland slaying of Al Capone's rivals in the notorious St. Valentine's Day Massacre, successfully tracing and identifying one of the Thompson submachine guns used in the murder to its owner, a gangster named Fred Burke who was duly arrested and charged afterwards. Goddard remained in Chicago, becoming the director of what at the time became the most advanced forensic analysis center in the United States—the Northwestern University Crime Laboratory.

All the forensic sciences had a rapid but painful growth and evolution over the last 150 years, from the ubiquitous fingerprint evidence, to blood stain analysis, fiber identification, forensic anthropology in victim identification, photo analysis, to the amazing science of DNA analysis that only blossomed within our own lifetimes recently. The science of blood analysis for example, had to progress from first the ability to identify stains as blood or not; then whether it is human or animal blood; later the blood type; and recently, since

DNA analysis (since the 1980s), to the precise individual.

This volume, RJ Parker's *Forensic Analysis and DNA in Criminal Investigations: Including Cold Cases Solved,* explores the recent evolution and 'state of the art' in forensic analysis in the twentieth and twenty-first centuries and illustrates in case studies how forensic sciences were essential in solving some of the most controversial crimes of the centuries.

The History of DNA and Forensic Analysis: *An Introduction to DNA*

DNA is the name prescribed to a molecule of nucleic acid that is essential to the functioning of the human body. DNA[i] stands for deoxyribonucleic acid, and this molecule is what is responsible for the encoding and relaying of genetic instructions from one generation to the next. DNA is also the single greatest biological signature that any creature possesses. It is what sets us apart from one another more than anything else, more so even than our famously unique fingerprints.

The structure of DNA is also a singularly unique portion of our biological make up. First and foremost, in most living organisms a strand of DNA is not a single molecule, but rather two molecules that are in a way fused to each other; in essence two strands of DNA that are wound around each other in a structure made famous in several medically-based movies called the double helix. DNA is found within the cells of living organisms, in long structures called chromosomes. The information present within this DNA, within these chromosomes, is how the cell instinctively knows how to perform the task it is meant for.

For example, a cell found in the lung is responsible for respiration. It uses glucose, which is obtained from the food one eats as the energy source for the activities it must perform. The cell in question instinctively knows that it must use glucose as its energy source for an activity that it also instinctively knows how to perform because the information stored within its chromosome tells it all it needs to know. This information is a form of genetic memory; it does not have to be learned—it only needs to be accessed by the cell.

The history of research regarding DNA[ii] can be traced back to the 1930s, when the field of molecular biology began to make some headway in the world of science. As the importance of molecular biology grew, we retreated within ourselves in an attempt to discover more about who we are, about where we came from, and we expanded upon several fields of science that came together to form this particular discipline. Specifically, these fields include biochemistry, genetics, microbiology, virology as well as physics. However, research into DNA only began to occur after the fact; that is to say, after scientists had actually discovered DNA.

The discovery of DNA occurred several decades before the various biological disciplines came together to form molecular biology. Ironically, the discovery of DNA can't be traced back to a science lab in the traditional sense. This is to say that DNA was not discovered in the sterile science lab that has been made so famous by countless depictions in film. Rather, it was discovered in the more rustic science lab of the farm. Genetics as a rough theory was well known among farmers familiar with genetic traits from what they witnessed in their own crops and livestock.

The father of genetics, the man that was responsible for the discovery of DNA, was a scientist by the name of Gregor Mendel. A rather interesting fact about this man is that he was not just a man of Science; he was a man of God as well. Born to a German family in the Austrian empire, Mendel became a man of the cloth in order to fund his education. While studying at the University of Olomouc, Mendel became fascinated by the variations found in plants of the same species. This is what led him to begin studying genetics.

Mendel's research was focused mainly on pea plants,[iii] with a particular emphasis on the seven traits of pea plants he felt were inherited separately from the rest of the traits that the plant possessed. The seven traits he studied included the shape of the seed, the color of the flower, the tint of the coat of the seed, the shape of the pod, the color of the unripe pod, the location of the flower and, finally, the height of the plant when it was fully grown. Mendel placed emphasis on the shape of the seed, which he found to be either angular and possessing sharp corners or round and smooth.

Over the seven years in which Mendel conducted this study, humanity's first true foray into genetic science, he ended up growing and conducting research on nearly thirty thousand pea plants, a remarkable number by any means, that truly signifies the scale at which research must be conducted to facilitate even the smallest breakthrough. After conducting his landmark research, Mendel came up with what would eventually come to be known as Mendel's Law of Inheritance, a law that would come to define the way humans perceive their own biology and the traits that we pass on to each younger generation.

When Mendel presented his papers to the members of the Society of Natural History in his hometown, his findings were initially viewed with much favour. However, when his work was finally published, many were under the misconception that the paper was about hybridization rather than a breakthrough on inheritance, and it was largely ignored. Today, the research is now considered Mendel's *magnum opus*, a seminal work and indeed the genesis of the field of genetics.

It is interesting to note that due to the fact that Mendel's research was largely ignored[iv] during his lifetime, a singularly important individual in the field of genetics, one that unwittingly used Mendelian science to discover the theory of evolution itself, was also unaware of the research. This man was named Charles Darwin. It is often speculated that if Darwin had read the research, it might have sparked a scientific revolution. This revolution would have probably resulted in the birth of the field of genetics several decades before it eventually came into vogue as science caught up to Mendel's research.

Regardless of what could have been, the field of genetics wallowed at the precipice of becoming a full-fledged scientific discipline for the next few decades. During this time, an important new scientific discipline began to develop, a discipline known as cytology or the study of cells. As the cells of a living organism began to be studied in greater detail, the scientific community was able to use this new knowledge to gain an understanding of the theories that Mendel had put forward in his published work. This facilitated a growth of interest regarding inheritance of traits and genetics.

One major event in the field of genetics that occurred a few years after Gregor Mendel published his research regarding genetic inheritance was the first instance in which DNA was isolated. This event occurred around six years after Mendel concluded his research. In the year 1969, a Swiss physician and biologist by the name Johannes Friedrich Miescher, while researching the chemistry of the nuclei of cells at the laboratory of Felix Hoppe-Seyler at the University of Tubingen in Germany, came across some trouble while attempting to remove pus from used bandages for the purposes of analyzing their biochemical structure.

Miescher was attempting to examine pus because it is full of leucocytes, or white blood cells, which were the type of cells he was focusing on. In order to remove the pus from the bandages without damaging the precious cells contained within, Miescher placed the bandages in a sodium sulfate solution and let them soak. The cells would then separate from the pus and settle at the bottom of the container. After isolating the nuclei of these cells via alkaline extraction followed by a process of acidification, Miescher discovered a substance that he referred to as nuclein in his published works.

This substance that he named nuclein was nucleic acid, a protein that the entire scientific community now refers to as DNA. Years later when the field of microbiology was proposed, the combination of Mendel's research leading to the law of genetic inheritance was linked to

Miescher's discovery of nucleic acid containing genetic information. As a result, the importance of both discoveries, each of them misunderstood as redundant research in the case of Mendel and an oddity in the case of Miescher, was finally realized. In a lot of ways, the link between these two discoveries is what eventually led to the creation of microbiology as a true field of science.

Warren Weaver of the Rockefeller Foundation first coined the term molecular biology in 1938. Thanks to advances within various fields of science, such as a realization of the importance of the theory of heredity based on the Mendelian chromosome, advancements made in the field of atomic theory, along with quantum mechanics in the previous decade led to the realization of a long-time scientific aspiration of many within the field to examine life in both physical and chemical dimensions at a microscopic level.

The 1930s and 1940s encompassed a period of nascence for the field of microbiology. The importance of DNA in the understanding of the way inheritance works, of the way the body functions, was clear, but the scientific community was unsure about how exactly they would delve deeper into the subject. No other use was seen for DNA, and the field of micro-biology and genetic science during these two decades was little more than speculation and hypothesizing based on pre-existing research. The breakthrough seemed just a step away, but the members of the scientific community simply didn't know the direction to take that step.

A couple of breakthroughs did occur in the 1940s regarding the understanding of the way DNA works within us, even if nobody yet knew that there could someday be a potential use for it outside of researching the human body. The first major breakthrough occurred in the year 1940 when George Beadle and Edward Tatum discovered that a precise relationship existed between genes and protein, which by proxy led to the second biggest discovery during this decade.

DNA is made up of nucleic acid, which is essentially a protein. Hence, the discovery of a direct link between genes and DNA led to a second discovery made by Oswald Avery approximately four years later. Avery, after an extensive period of research with much trial and error, discovered and eventually demonstrated that genes were entirely made up of DNA. Within a twenty-five year period, the field of microbiology made several important discoveries regarding DNA and how it worked, but the field became more or less stagnant after this. However, fifteen years later, technology finally caught up to the research and thus the field of genetic engineering, now an important part of science, was born.

This was the beginning of a veritable boom as far as DNA was concerned. Since Gregor Mendel's discovery, scientists had been examining, analyzing, and conducting tireless research on the way DNA works. However, this was done from within a veneer of scientific curiosity, of theoretical analysis of an entity integral to the functioning of our bodies and the continued growth of an entire species, for the purposes of better understanding it and, by extension, ourselves and the world around us. Never before was the concept of engineering ever thought to be compatible with an entity so delicate as DNA.

Yes, as human ingenuity would so often

have it, when a thing has been understood in a most thorough manner, it is the nature of man to attempt to alter that thing and shape it. When the entity that has been fully understood is a thing so fundamental to the functioning of virtually every living organism that does and ever will exist, a thing such as DNA that shapes the functioning of said organisms piece by piece and cell by cell, then humanity was inevitably going to bring itself to a point where it would be able to control said entity.

Eventually, DNA began to be used in several different fields, many of which have absolutely nothing to do with science as a means of conducting theoretical research. In fact, the manipulation and examination of DNA began to take on a far more practical method of use when its importance came to be fully understood. The fact that DNA is present in virtually every part of a human being, be it the person's hair, blood, saliva, or any other bodily fluid, means that it is extremely easy to obtain and thus became very commonly used for several purposes.

Genetic engineering itself began to take on a very godlike demeanour, with genetic scientists starting to manipulate DNA in order to improve various aspects of human life. This was done in several ways, one of the most important of which was the development of cures for genetic ailments that were previously considered untreatable lifelong sentences of pain and suffering. Genetic engineering eventually came to a point where hereditary illnesses could at least be discovered in children before they were born, or in the parents of the child, if either of them possessed any recessive traits, which would in turn facilitate a more informed and hence easier life for the child.

Another important way that genetic engineering is now used for the betterment of mankind is in the genetic modification of food. The world is slowly becoming extremely overcrowded, and as a result, a shortage of food is a perpetual cause for concern. Genetic modification of seeds can allow farmers to grow crops without worrying about pests or blights resulting in a low harvest, as the food is genetically modified to be resistant to such things. As a result, the worldwide shortage of food has started to abate. While the genetic modification of food has led to a lot of controversy, with many people considering it to be against religious norms, this does not detract from the fact that the manipulation of DNA has resulted in a huge amount of progress in many fields.

The way DNA works has also allowed it to be used for several other purposes. Although DNA is generally a device of sorts in which biological information is stored, the intrepidity of human science has brought it out of the field of biology completely and has begun using it as something completely different: a structural material.

In the field of DNA-based nanotechnology, DNA is used to create other materials that are used for a variety of purposes. The technology created in this branch of science, such as a nanotube, is used to conduct experiments in structural physics and chemistry, as the mo-lecular size of such technology allows it to be used in places too small for anything else. DNA is also used in this field to construct DNA computers and molecular machines, which are making real headway in the field of computer science.

Interestingly, the scientific community has taken note of DNA's ability to store biological information and got the idea to use the material to store computer data as well. In the year 2013, a group of scientists managed to store 719 kilobytes of information in a single sequence of DNA, which, when they relayed and decoded the data from the DNA sequence, they discovered it was stored with a hundred percent accuracy. Considering the microscopic size of a single strand of DNA and the nascence of this technology, the potential for this method of storing information is vast.

The examination, analysis, and manipulation of DNA is also used in fields totally unrelated to any form of science and technology in the traditional sense. Indeed, DNA has become singularly important to a branch of human knowledge that is far from the cold, sterile laboratory setting that one tends to envision when thinking of scientific analysis. This branch of human knowledge is known as the humanities, and is essentially an examination of a human being, not as a biological entity, but as a being of heritage and history, the study of humanities past, and the study of our biological relationships to one another.

Two branches of humanities in particular make great use of DNA. These two branches are history and anthropology. In the studying of our past and where we came from, along with the examination of how we relate to each other on a biological level, these two branches of humanities are intrinsically intertwined, particularly in how useful DNA is to the object of their research. DNA can be extracted from any reasonably preserved remnant of an ancient human being. Extracting this DNA and comparing it can teach us a lot about where the populations of entire nations came from, the migratory patterns of our ancestors, and above all, the way that human beings have interacted throughout history and how these interactions affect the way we behave now.

This extraction and comparison of DNA is not just important to the two branches of humanities that have been discussed. A rather different use for DNA has absolutely nothing to do with science, technology, or research of any kind, but this usage might be the single most practical thing that anyone can use DNA for as it deals with the safeguarding of human lives and the maintaining of law and order.

The usage of DNA analysis in criminal investigative procedure is known as forensic science. Blood, saliva, hair, or skin that is discovered at crime scenes can be used to extract DNA from. This DNA can then be compared to DNA collected from persons suspected of committing the crime in question in a procedure that is known as DNA profiling or genetic fingerprinting, in a reference to the time-honoured usage of fingerprints to convict criminals of their crimes. The benefit of using DNA in criminal investigative procedure is that it is extremely reliable, which means that there is no better way of at least proving that a suspect was at the scene of the crime.

Another incredibly important and sometimes overlooked usage for DNA analysis in criminal incidents is the identification of victims whose facial features are rendered indiscernible by the nature of the crime that was committed against them. A common victim type that is often identified using DNA analysis is the burn victim. Victims of mass casualties are also often identified using DNA analysis, such as the victims of a plane crash or some type of gas explosion.

DNA analysis is also often used to identify victims of warfare that were disposed of in mass graves. Many casualties of war have been identified using some form of DNA analysis that matched the casualty to a family member. Hence, there are several uses for DNA analysis in this particular area. However, it is the opinion of many that the single finest use for DNA analysis since genetic engineering first allowed us to isolate and individually examine DNA is its use in criminal investigative procedure. The sheer accuracy of this method of linking suspected perpetrators to the scenes of their crimes has resulted in a veritable revolution in the world of criminal investigation.

This is the aspect of DNA and its analysis that will be analyzed in this book. The impact of DNA on criminal investigative procedure and profiling will also be discussed, as well as the accuracy of DNA as evidence. Furthermore, the frequency in which criminals are apprehended using this method of identification will also be examined, along with any instances in which DNA analysis proved to be wrong or hindered the criminal justice system in any way. An overall discussion of forensic science, its history and its eventual use of DNA, is up next.

A History of Forensic Science

Forensics is a term[v] used to describe a linkage of sorts between two highly different fields. These two fields are criminal investigative procedure as well as scientific analysis. The field of forensics essentially involves taking a scientific approach to the procedure of criminal investigation through gathering of empirical evidence, the objective analysis of said evidence, and the presentation of the information gathered from this evidence in a court of law, essentially allowing criminal investigators as well as prosecutors to prove the presence of a potential suspect at the scene of a crime.

The need for forensic science[vi] stemmed from an inability to connect criminals to the scene of the crime. When a man kills another man with no witnesses to point the finger at him, what can the person investigating the murder do about it? A dependence on confession as well as witness testimony led to a terrible system in which people were coerced to confess to crimes they didn't commit, forced to bear witness when they saw nothing, and all of it resulted in the vast majority of criminals walking free without facing any kind of penalty whatsoever.

Proof of use of certain primitive methods[vii] of forensic analysis can be found in ancient Indian and Chinese cultures, where people suspected of committing a crime were required to fill up their mouths with dried rice for a period of time before spitting it out. The theory behind this was that if a person were guilty, the rice would end up sticking to his or her mouth in large quantities. A similar primitive, and somewhat brutal, forensic method was used in ancient Middle Eastern cultures, where a person suspected of a crime was required to briefly place their tongue against a hot piece of metal. It was believed if the person were guilty, the metal would burn the tongue. However, the hot metal would do them no harm if they were innocent.

The science behind each of these methods is sound to a certain extent. In theory, someone that is lying would have less saliva in his or her mouth. Rice would end up sticking to the inside of a dry mouth, whereas a mouth full of saliva would prevent large amounts of rice from adhering to its inner surface. As for the hot metal test, a coating of saliva would prevent one's tongue from getting burnt for a very short period of time. When people lie, their mouths tends to get very dry, which would result in a burned tongue when taking this test.

It is fairly easy to see the flaws in these proto-forensic crime investigation techniques. One's mouth can get dry due to anxiety as well, and it is highly understandable for an individual to get dry mouth when accused of a crime he did not commit, or, worse still, if he had to press his tongue against a red-hot piece of metal to prove his innocence! Hence, there was too much of a margin of error involved in these techniques for them to be taken seriously as the human species advanced.

There is, however, an example of forensic analysis conducted in ancient times, although this event likely took place long after the aforementioned proto-forensic techniques lost favour among the ancient societies that practiced them. This instance of a form of forensic science being used to solve a crime can be considered in many ways to be an early breakthrough in the field of forensics, one that occurred not just centuries, but millennia, before forensic science was actually standardized and integrated into criminal investigative procedure.

This instance of forensic methodology that was so far ahead of its time occurred in Greece roughly two-and-a-half centuries before the Common Era. During this time, Greece was making new strides in the way knowledge was perceived and obtained. This was mainly because the Kingdom of Greece was one of the main influences for the formidable Roman Empire and Alexander's empire. The descendants of these people would go far and wide to spread the old Greek philosophy, emphasizing on knowledge, logic, and rationale in other countries that the Romans and Macedonians conquered. At one point, they had control of virtually eighty percent of the modern world.

This event that occurred approximately two-and-a-half centuries before the Common Era was related to a rather simple offence, one that could arguably even be called rather minor. The King of Greece during this time was a man named Hiero the Second. Hiero had provided a blacksmith with a certain amount of gold and had commissioned said blacksmith to make him a crown using the entirety of the gold provided.

When the king received his crown, he was doubtful about the honesty of the blacksmith, feeling as though he had mixed a small amount of silver in with the gold to make the crown feel as heavy as pure gold and had pocketed the gold that was saved as a result. The weight of the crown was equivalent to the weight of the gold that the blacksmith had received, yet Hiero was still not convinced of the man's honesty. Unsure of how to judge the man, nor of how to prove whether he was innocent or guilty, Hiero decided to approach a great thinker for help in the matter. This thinker was a great philosopher and mathematician by the name of Archimedes.

When Hiero approached Archimedes for help in solving the problem, he told the philosopher that he could not melt the crown down to ascertain its properties, as it was simply too valuable. As melting the crown and separating its elements would have been an easy way to solve this problem, the conditions placed upon him by his king left Archimedes with a puzzle to solve with what seemed like a piece or two missing. However, being the great philosopher, logical thinker and problem solver that he was, Archimedes did not let the difficulty of the task discourage him in any way.

In his contemplation of the puzzle he was tasked to solve, it is said that Archimedes eventually became frustrated and decided to take a relaxing bath, approach the problem with a fresh mind, and possibly find a new angle from which to look at it. As he entered his bath and descended into the water, Archimedes noticed something curious and utterly intriguing. As more of his body entered the water, the level of the water seemed to rise higher. All of a sudden, the man's great mind saw the link between the rising bath water and the problem that he had been asked to solve by his king. In his utter elation, Archimedes shouted his now famous phrase, "Eureka!"

So delighted was Archimedes that he had solved this seemingly unsolvable problem, in such ecstasy was he after receiving that moment of inspiration that allowed him to solve a problem that seemed to have no solution based in any form of logic, that he ran through the streets of Athens naked as the day he was born across the entire city to deliver the good news to his king.

Or so the legend goes, as narrated by Vitruvius, a noted Roman author. This rather fantastical version of the tale is probably mostly exaggeration for the sake of making the narrative more interesting, but the basic premise of this event is based firmly in history and is the first recorded instance of any individual using a method of ostensibly forensic or scientific nature in order to prove the guilt of someone that had committed a crime almost two millennia before such a thing would become commonplace in the modern criminal justice system.

The moment of inspiration that Archimedes received was the realization of one thing that could determine whether the blacksmith was honest or not: density. No matter what the weight of the object was, its density would vary. For example, a pound of silver is far less dense than a pound of gold, even though both of the metals possess the exact same weight, something known to the ancient Greeks in a somewhat primitive way.

The density of an object can be measured by placing it in water and measuring how much the water rises. Using this technique, one can at the very least compare the densities of two different materials even if one is unable to ascertain the exact density of each object. According to the legend, Archimedes was reminded of this concept when he submerged himself in his bath, although it is far more likely he had his eureka moment as a result of extensive objective analysis of empirically collected evidence and the whole story involving the bath is probably no more than fiction.

Gold weighing the same amount as the crown was placed into a container full of water. The point to which the water rose was marked. After the gold was extracted, the crown was subsequently submerged in the water. If the crown had been made of gold, as an honest blacksmith would have ensured, the water would have risen roughly the same amount. However, the water rose significantly less than before, proving the blacksmith had mixed some silver into the crown in order to steal whatever gold he ended up saving as a result of his forgery.

It is unknown what happened to the blacksmith when he was proved guilty of this crime, but the utter ingenuity with which Archimedes solved this problem was indicative of how examination of evidence, as well as rational thinking, would come to shape the way crime would be solved far into the future when the field of forensics would eventually be developed. Even though the method Archimedes used was primitive, its use displayed the first recorded example of knowledge and reasoning being used to solve a crime rather than dependence on confession and testimony, both of which can and have been forcefully obtained.

This instance of forensic-like methodology being used to solve a crime was unique in a time when rather barbaric methods were being used to arbitrarily deem people innocent or guilty.

It can be argued that Archimedes's use of forensic deduction to solve the crime was the result of mere happenstance. This is true, as the genesis of scientific methodology being deliberately used in the process of criminal investigation was still many centuries away. The genesis of science being intentionally used to solve crime was still rather far from this instance in terms of both time and distance. Whereas the first recorded instance of forensic-like techniques were recorded in Greece two-and-a-half centuries before the Common Era, the first properly researched and published work discussing the proliferation of forensic techniques would be written about a millennia-and-a-half later, all the way across the world.

This published work is a book titled *Xi Yuan Lu*,[viii] which is the name it possesses in the language it was written: Chinese. A rough translation of this name would be "The Washing Away of Wrongdoing." In the book written by Song Ci (1186–1249), possibly one of the earliest examples of a true forensic expert, several criminal cases are discussed at length. It is in the discussion of these criminal cases that the first examples of intentional usage of forensic techniques are used to solve crimes.[ix]

One such example is in the case of a man

having been murdered in a village. Upon examination of the wounds suffered by the victim, and the comparison of these wounds to those suffered by several animals, the investigators were able to determine the murder weapon that had been used was a sickle. Using this knowledge, the investigators were able to determine who the murderer was through a rather clever technique that tied the murderer to the scene of the crime.

The use of a sickle narrowed down the list of potential perpetrators, as it indicated that a peasant had likely committed the murder. Peasants used sickles to harvest rice, and so would be the people most likely to have a sickle on hand to commit the crime. Knowing this, the magistrate in charge of bringing the murderer to justice rounded up all the suspects and told them to place their sickles out in front of them and step back. Within a few minutes, blowflies began to descend onto one of the sickles, ignoring all of the other ones. Eventually, the owner of the sickle, realizing that the attention from the blowflies would prove that he was guilty, broke down and confessed to his crimes. The magistrate was quite clever using this technique. He was well aware that a sickle used in the murder, no matter how well it was cleaned, would still have blood, tissue, and hair on it. Though more or less invisible to the naked eye, it would still draw the attention of blowflies, which were attracted to carcasses as well as rotting and dead meat.

This passage in this book about forensic methodology is extremely important for two reasons. First and foremost, it involved the examination of the body of a murder victim to ascertain as much information as possible about how the individual died. This indicated the magistrate's knowledge of the importance of the visual details of a victim, and how those details could reveal important clues about the perpetrator of the murder, including his murder weapon and modus operandi.

The second reason that this passage is important is because it is one of the oldest written accounts in which forensic methodology was used to ascertain the murder weapon and how this was used to narrow down the list of suspects. The methods discussed in this passage would eventually become mainstays of forensic methodology when the branch of science would become integral to the criminal investigative process many centuries later. Song Ci's book is, in this sense, incredibly influential as it contains more specifically forensic investigative methods, improving distinctly on Archimedes's more proto-forensic methodology.

Apart from important passages like this, Song Ci's book is extremely important in the history of forensic science as it outlines a detailed etiquette for forensic scientists and coroners to follow, etiquette that in many ways defines the way coroners treat the bodies of murder victims today. Song Ci particularly emphasized the coroner's responsibility, talking at great length about how it was the duty of the coroner to bear the stench of the corpse and examine it with his or her own eyes rather than making a subordinate do it, and how it was important for coroners to fill in the details of their autopsies themselves.

The entire purpose of Song Ci's book can be ascertained from the tone with which it was written. Song Ci admired, almost revered, the science of forensics. The book seems to have been written as if its purpose were to prevent injustices and false convictions, two things that were extremely common before the popularization of forensic methodology in criminal investigative procedure. In this book, which is alternatively titled *"Collected Cases of Injustice Rectified,"* Song Ci writes about how it is essential for coroners and forensic scientists to take their jobs seriously, else they would be committing egregious injustices against both the deceased as well as the person punished for the crime if they have been wrongly convicted.

This philosophy of Song Ci greatly influenced the way forensic science developed over the next few years. His book was very well received upon its release and is still highly regarded by those involved in forensic analysis. A good indicator of the popularity of his book is that it has been translated into seven languages and it is still a popular buy today, almost eight centuries later.

As science as an overall discipline continued to advance, the field of forensic science began to make some real headway in the west some time in the fifteenth century. A number of European doctors and surgeons conducted some important research into forensic methodology in the years between the fifteenth to seventeenth centuries. One of the first Europeans to study the changes brought about to the human body after a violent death was a French surgeon by the name of Ambroise Pare. Two Italian surgeons, Fortunato Fidelis and Paola Zacchia, also studied the structural changes brought about to the human body after disease had struck, laying the foundations for pathology, a branch of medicine closely linked to forensic science.

However, it was not until the eighteenth century that the hypothesis and conjecture of medical professionals on criminal investigative procedure began to be taken seriously. It was during this century that the first written works based on research into the usefulness of forensic analysis began to emerge. Hence, as published works on the subject began appearing, the criminal justice system began taking forensic science a lot more seriously than it had before.

The reason for the huge gap between the writings of Song Ci and the development and proliferation of forensic methodology in the west is quite interesting. Despite the fact that Archimedes was virtually a westerner and his method of thinking really should have been popularized due to its methodology, Europe seemed to drift into a veritable dark age of criminal justice procedure. As a Chinese magistrate practically wrote the book on forensic etiquette and usefulness, Europeans continued to use torture to induce confessions. It seems like Archimedes's eureka moment was just an anomaly and the world wasn't ready for such rational solutions just yet.

But, in the eighteenth century, all of this began to change. This is due to the fact that the eighteenth century fell in the middle of what is now called the Age of Enlightenment.[x] During this era, western ideology began to undergo a paradigm shift. Suddenly the intellectuals of the west began to realize and proliferate the importance of reason and logic over unquestioned and unchecked authoritarianism, finally catching up to Ancient Greece in a way. As people began to question themselves and the things they did, the traditional elements, such as confessions under duress, were seen to be ineffectual.

This led to an increased interest in forensic methodology. Use of torture was mostly ceased, and all forms of superstitious belief began to stop influencing the decisions made by the criminal justice system. A once highly ineffectual system that arbitrarily assigned guilt as it saw fit soon began to take its first few tentative steps into the light of reason and, in doing so, began using forensic methodology in the apprehension and conviction of those suspected of committing some kind of crime.

As the methodology of forensic analysis began to increase in popularity, two distinct cases occurred within a span of roughly thirty years, which can be seen as examples of how popular forensic science was becoming in England during this time. The first of these two cases occurred close to the end of the eighteenth century, the century in which authoritarianism[xi] began to give way to rational thought allowing forensic methodology to flourish, in 1784 to be precise, whereas the second case occurred a little over thirty years later in the year 1816.

The first case occurred in Lancashire and involved the murder of a man named Edward Culshaw. The culprit was eventually apprehended, a man by the name of John Toms, through the use of forensic techniques. Investigators examined Culshaw's body and found a pistol wad, which is essentially a torn piece of paper used to seal the gunpowder and bullet in the muzzle of the gun, in the head wound that had resulted in his death. This pistol wad was discovered to be from the newspaper that the investigators had found in John Toms's pocket, successfully tying the man to the murder he had committed.

The second major case that was solved as a result of an increased interest in forensic methodology occurred in Warwick. A young maidservant bearing the marks of a violent assault had been found drowned in a shallow pool. Investigators examined the crime scene and discovered grains of wheat and chaff scattered across the ground. From this they gleaned that the perpetrator of this murder had been a farm labourer. Further examination of the crime scene led the investigators to discover a shoe print. Matching this shoe print to a farm labourer working nearby allowed the investigators to successfully convict a man that had murdered an innocent young girl in cold blood.

It can be plainly seen from the two afore-mentioned cases that logic and problem solving were now becoming staples of the criminal investigative procedure. England was finally catching up to Archimedes. However, a separate branch of forensic science had begun developing in the eighteenth century, one that dealt not with rational thought but with chemistry. Chemistry is now one of the most important aspects of forensic methodology, so one can imagine just how integral this advancement became during this time.

Throughout history, poisoning has always proved to be a very tricky way to kill somebody. Certainly there are very obvious poisons out there, poisons that work with absolutely no subtlety, leaving proof of the fact that the victim had been poisoned all over the body. However, there still exist several poisons that can kill individuals without much outward indication of foul play. Whatever the case may be, there had never in history been a way to detect if a person had been poisoned if he or she showed no outward signs that a toxic substance had entered his or her system.

All of this changed in the eighteenth century, in the year 1773, when a Swedish physicist by the name of Carl Wilhelm Scheele[xii] devised a way to find out if a corpse contained unusually large amounts of arsenic. A positive result would indicate that the victim had been poisoned prior to death, although the test could not confirm whether the ingestion of the poison itself was the actual cause of death or not. This marked the very first time that poison could be detected inside the body of someone that was already dead!

A little more than thirty years later, Scheele's method was researched and improved on by a German chemist by the name of Valentin Ross. The improvements that Ross made to Scheele's method was to broaden its horizons, allowing chemists to detect poison not just in the contents of the stomach of a victim, but also in the lining of the stomach itself. This allows for the detection of far more subtle poisons that dissipate quickly from the contents of the stomach. Any residue remaining on the lining of the stomach allowed coroners to identify what caused the victim's death.

Although these discoveries weren't initially

intended to be used in the criminal investigative procedure, in the year 1832, when forensic methodology was starting to gain popularity in the justice system of England, a chemist by the name of John Marsh became the first man to apply chemical theory to forensic methodology. When called as a witness at the trial of a man accused of poisoning his father, Marsh used this test to prove that the man had arsenic in his system, thereby proving foul play. However, despite the fact that Marsh was able to prove that there was arsenic present in the victim's system, the jury acquitted the perpetrator due to the fact that the arsenic had deteriorated.

This failure to help put a man guilty of murder behind bars spurred Marsh to improve the method by which poison could be detected in the body of a victim. His research resulted in some major improvements in the test, where chemists were soon able to detect even extremely minute traces of arsenic in the body of a recently deceased person. Trace amounts as miniscule as one-fiftieth of a gram of arsenic could be detected in his test, greatly improving its credibility.

Around the same time Marsh was developing an extremely sophisticated way to determine whether or not someone had been killed through arsenic poisoning, another extremely important discovery was being made by an individual named Henry Goddard,[xiii] who worked for Scotland Yard at the time. This discovery was the creation of bullet comparison, a forensic technique that has greatly improved the chances of catching a shooter and putting him behind bars. Goddard came up with the idea for bullet comparison after tracing a defective bullet used to kill somebody back to its manufacturer's mould, which eventually led him to the killer.

With all of this progress being made in England, one could easily believe that modern forensic methodology was born and matured entirely in the United Kingdom. However, this simply wasn't the case. Major discoveries and breakthroughs were also being made across the English Channel in France. In fact, it is in France that an entire field of forensic science developed, thanks to the presence of one man who can safely be considered one of the fathers of modern forensic science: Alphonse Bertillon.

Before the 1870s, when Alphonse Bertillon[xiv] began advancing the field of forensic science in leaps and bounds, the only way to identify a criminal was through photographic evidence or a name. It is clear to see why this was so ineffectual, as photographs weren't readily available in the nineteenth century and names can always be faked. Frustrated by the inefficient means by which criminals were being identified, Bertillon decided to finally take matters into his own hands and change this "catch-as-catch-can" methodology of the French justice system by developing a superior method for human classification.

This system of human classification is a branch of forensic methodology known as anthropometry. This basically involves documenting the measurements of every criminal that is apprehended, from their height to their weight. This allowed criminals to become recognizable in ways apart from their face, such as their height and girth. This was the first example of human classification being used in forensic methodology, something that would eventually become a mainstay in the criminal investigative procedure. Anthropometry revolutionized the way criminals were classified, but despite its greatness, it turned out to be just the first of Bertillon's many forensic innovations.

Bertillon developed a material that would be able to preserve footprints, allowing these useful pieces of evidence to be treated as such and examined at length rather than being quickly looked at on the crime scene before becoming contaminated by the police working the case. He also took Goddard's bullet comparison idea and expanded on it greatly, inventing much of the groundwork that would go into the modern day ballistics forensic investigative technique. Bertillon also invented several pieces of forensic equipment, such as the dynamometer, which could be used to find out how much force had been used during a break in.

Although many of his innovations eventually became obsolete, such as the modern day preference of fingerprinting over anthropometry, Bertillon was possibly the first great innovator in the field of forensic science. Even though many of his inventions fell out of favour, some of his inventions are still used today such as the mug shot and the methodology used by modern-day crime scene photographers in order to maintain the integrity of the crime scene, proving just how far ahead of his time Bertillon truly was.

In the last two to three decades of the nineteenth century, perhaps the single greatest innovation in the history of forensic science was invented and developed. This invention would come to define the human classification system that Bertillon tried so hard to build, completing the dream that he had that would allow police to successfully classify criminals and be able to identify them later on. This innovation was the use of fingerprints to identify people, based on the discovery that fingerprints were the single most unique aspect about every human being.

The use of fingerprints can be traced as far back as Sir William Herschel,[xv] who began to use fingerprints to prove his identity after his signature was repeatedly rejected due to discrepancies. After about twenty years of advocating the use of fingerprints, Herschel began to implement fingerprinting to prevent relatives of pensioners from collecting money after the original recipient's death and to confirm the

identity of prisoners after sentencing to prevent convicted felons from avoiding jail time.
That marked the first time in history fingerprints were used for any purpose in the criminal justice system.

Herschel's advocacy for the use of fingerprinting to identify people was validated by a
Scottish doctor by the name of Henry Faulds.
Faulds[xvi] holds the distinction of publishing the
first research paper in which taking fingerprints
is proposed as a reliable method for identifying
people. He also proposed what ink to use
when taking fingerprints (printing ink) and was
the first person in history to identify someone
based on a fingerprint that they left. Faulds'
research took place in Tokyo, and when he returned to London, he approached the London
Metropolitan Police with his idea, but they
dismissed it.

A cousin of Charles Darwin's, a man by the
name of Francis Galton, was approached by
Faulds to help validate the reliability of using
fingerprints. An anthropologist by profession,
Galton was so inspired by this concept that he
studied it for an entire decade after realizing
that the chance of two people sharing a set of

fingerprints was one in sixty-four billion. Over the next ten years, Galton compiled a statistical model for fingerprint analysis,[xvii] which he published under the title *Finger Prints*, along with strong recommendations to apply this concept in law enforcement.

This published work ended up being the straw that broke the camel's back as far as fingerprinting was concerned. As a result of reading the book, a police inspector in Argentina, Juan Vucetich, set up the world's first fingerprint bureau in the year 1892. The usefulness of fingerprint analysis can be seen in the very same year that the fingerprint bureau was opened, as the use of the bureau and comparative fingerprint analysis allowed police officers to apprehend a murderer that had been trying to frame an innocent person for the crimes that he had committed.

In 1892, in the city of Necochea, a woman by the name of Francisca Rojas[xviii] was found in her home, having sustained neck injuries, next to the dead bodies of her two sons. Rojas accused her neighbour of murdering her children, but the neighbour refused to confess to the crime even after extreme interrogation techniques were used. One of the investigators saw a bloody fingerprint at the crime scene and decided to compare it to Rojas's fingerprint. The result was a match, proving that Rojas committed filicidal murder against her sons. The woman only confessed after her guilt was proven, something that would never have happened if fingerprinting hadn't been conceived.

This case is extremely important to the history of forensic science, as it is the first ever instance of a criminal being apprehended due to the presence of a fingerprint from the scene of a crime. The apprehension of a single criminal was proof that fingerprinting could work as a system of human classification, and slowly but surely, Alphonse Bertillon's anthropometrics system began to decline in popularity in favour of the far more accurate and reliable fingerprinting system. The very next fingerprint bureau that would open would be indicative of the future of human classification.

In the next five years after the first successful arrest using fingerprints, the system began to gain popularity in an unofficial capacity. A major breakthrough occurred when the Council of the Governor General of India[xix] decided to start using fingerprints as a way to classify criminal records. A department was set up in Calcutta's Anthropometrics Bureau, but with fingerprints being so effective and reliable, the anthropometrics bureau eventually turned into the Fingerprints Bureau, another addition to the growing popularity of fingerprinting in the criminal justice system. The classification system used in this bureau was known as the Henry Classification System, and it is this system that the United Kingdom eventually adopted.

In 1901, more than twenty years after Henry Faulds had proposed the idea, Scotland Yard, along with the London Metropolitan Police, created the United Kingdom Fingerprint Bureau. Over the years, this system of classifying people through the use of fingerprints is estimated to have caught thousands of criminals, to the point where dusting for fingerprints is a stereotypical activity of the average investigative police officer. One can only imagine the progress that would have been achieved if the London Metropolitan Police had accepted Faulds's idea when he proposed it in the first place.

Not one to be left behind, the United States began implementing fingerprinting in its New York Civil Service. In 1906, Joseph A. Faurot, the deputy commissioner of the New York City Police Department[xx] and an avid fan of Bertillon's and long-time advocate of fingerprinting, made the New York City Police the first police department in the United States of America to begin fingerprinting criminals. As the twentieth century progressed, fingerprinting became the single most popular forensic method in the world.

With all of this attention that forensic science was getting, the true measure of its success was to be judged not through the amount of police forces adopting it, but from its depiction in popular culture, and for its part, forensic science, the new and exciting crime fighting technique that it was, certainly became quite famous as a magical way to know just who did the deed and exactly how they did it. Depictions in the modern day world are plentiful, but it is interesting to note that back in the late nineteenth century when forensic science was still gaining traction, forensic methodology was being introduced to the public at large through a series of very popular books.

The main character of these books is a name you might have heard of: Sherlock Holmes. The author of these novels, a man by the name of Sir Arthur Conan Doyle, seemed to have almost uncanny insight into the world of forensic investigative methodology, with his character speaking of many things barely being used by any police departments in the world, things such as fingerprints, the examination of trace evidence on items such as shoelaces, and the smell of gunpowder. Sherlock Holmes was also known to complain often about how the police officers that came to a crime scene would always end up contaminating it, something that was also very indicative of forensic methodology, although the practice of maintaining the integrity of crime scenes was not yet very popular in the world's police departments. Another forensic activity that this character performed before such an activity became popular anywhere else was handwriting analysis, along with ballistics analysis and analytical chemistry.

Virtually all the techniques used by Sherlock Holmes were still nascent at the times the novels were being written and published, barely used by any police departments of note in the world. Yet each and every one of the techniques that were used eventually became mainstays of the criminal investigative process.

This almost precognitive knowledge about forensic methodology before it became popular among the world's police captured the world's imagination, and probably helped greatly in the eventual popularization and standardization of forensic science in the various spheres of the criminal investigative process. Sherlock Holmes seemed like a magician, and when the police realized that they had the power in their hands to do what he did, they were inclined to act on their knowledge.

As the twentieth century progressed, forensic methodology became standard practice in most aspects of the criminal investigative process. The popularization of forensic science coincided with perhaps the single most famous case in history, which is also the single most important case in the history of forensic science as well. It is a watershed case in many ways, as it was the first instance in history when such a widespread investigation was conducted on such a large scale using exclusively forensic criminal investigative techniques.

The case that is being spoken of here is the infamous Jack the Ripper[xxi] case. In the 1880s, a series of murders occurred in the Whitechapel area in London. In the year 1888, five prostitutes were brutally murdered in the streets of this area, and the brutal nature of these crimes resulted in an utter media furor. London had always called itself the center of civilization, and the brutal murders that were happening right in its backyard under the very noses of its police force prompted a lot of media outlets to ridicule the city and the London Metropolitan Police department.

In order to apprehend the perpetrator of these murders and save face, Scotland Yard implemented all the forensic techniques that they had at their disposal. This marked the first instance where forensic materials were collected meticulously and the investigative officers in charge took great care in maintaining the integrity of the crime scene, something that had never been done before because crime scene integrity was just never taken all that seriously. The tailing of suspects also took on a very forensic and systematic approach, with each suspect being tailed and monitored until the police were sure of their innocence. It should be noted that this is the first time that a list of suspects had been made in such a manner, although the practice is commonplace in today's investigative procedure.

House-to-house inquiries were also held for the first time in history, even though the practice is widespread today, in an effort to speak to as many witnesses as possible. Experts estimate that upwards of two thousand people were interviewed, three hundred people were investigated, and almost a hundred were kept in custody for one reason or another.

Through forensic deduction, the Metropolitan Police Department of London hypothesized that the killer had to work as either a butcher or surgeon, due to the nature of the murders that were being committed. During the investigation, several butchers and surgeons were either called in for questioning or monitored closely. As a result of the intensive investigation, the officers in charge of the case were able to build a profile on the Ripper. They were able to ascertain through profiling techniques that the offender was reclusive but prone to fits of erotic mania in which he would commit these murders. The notes he was sending to the police office seemed to indicate he felt no remorse for what he had done, and that he also craved attention and recognition in whatever way he could get it. Religious extremism was suggested due to the nature of the victims being targeted, but that theory was soon scrapped.

Even though the investigators managed to create a profile on the offender, essentially detailing the *type* of man that the Ripper was, the investigation was ultimately unsuccessful. To this day, the killer remains unknown. However, it is still a landmark investigation because it set a precedent for how cases of such magnitude should be handled that is followed to this day with a lot more success.

Hence, the aforementioned passages are a discussion of two distinct events that ended up affecting public perspective and altering it to make forensic science a more palatable concept. No longer was forensic methodology an oddity with unproven results, nor were the different facets and techniques involved in this science unknown to the common folk anymore. Thanks to these two distinct events, these two phenomena of the late nineteenth century, forensic science and its methodology found its place in the criminal investigative process, taking root and spreading, slowly growing into the integral facet of criminology that it is today.

Sherlock Holmes is the first phenomenon that shifted public perception to a more favourable outlook on forensic methodology. The wild popularity of this series of books, along with the uncannily accurate forensic terminology and methodology contained therein, resulted in a wide proliferation of such concepts among the psyche of the public. Suddenly, there was a widespread public interest in forensic sciences, people knew and cared about the integrity of the crime scene, about the presence of trace evidence that might end up being the straw that broke the proverbial camel's back—the camel's back being the criminal case in question.

Since those involved in the criminal justice system are, in fact, members of the public themselves, their imagination was also captured by this near-magical way of producing results for an investigation. They saw forensic science being applied in these fictional, but barely so, novels and felt that this was a credible way to solve crime since everything depicted in these books was virtually on the precipice of being real. These novels showed people just what forensic science and methodology could do when applied to the criminal investigative process when allowed to flourish and when used to its fullest extent.

It can be argued that this first phenomenon, the publishing of a wildly popular book series that featured detailed forensic techniques being used, created a bit of leeway when forensic methodology failed to produce results in the second major phenomenon that resulted in the popularization of forensic methodology, which was the media furor that surrounded the Ripper case. The public at large was mostly ready to forgive the lack of results simply because they had seen something depicted so adventurously in fiction played out in real life, and they wanted more. Although Sherlock Holmes was fiction, the storytelling was so realistic that people were convinced such things could definitely happen in real life.

And so, with so much media attention during the last quarter of the nineteenth century, forensic science and methodology finally found its place firmly in the realm of criminal investigative procedure, as well as the criminal justice system. It was finally allowed to grow, and each forensic technique was expanded upon and improved until we finally received the myriad of forensic techniques we use today. The improvements in technology during the twentieth century greatly helped in improving the accuracy of forensic science in its application in criminal investigation. Proliferation of forensic technique allowed a lot of improvements to be made to forensic methodology as well. It allowed individuals to conduct trial and error experiments on a global scale, permitting forensic scientists to test the scope of their field and its techniques very quickly.

Possibly the single greatest appropriation of forensic methodology in the twentieth century was the creation of the Federal Bureau of Investigation in the United States of America. The FBI, as it is known in its abbreviated form, is the federal investigative authority of the

United States of America, which is above the jurisdictions of the relatively autonomous states that comprise this nation. The creator of the FBI was a man by the name of J. Edgar Hoover. The FBI was the first institution in the world that contained a central fingerprint database, and it in many ways standardized the forensic methodology that is used today. The FBI, along with its somewhat controversial founder and beginnings, will be discussed in detail in a later chapter.

In the twentieth century, several different branches of forensic science developed as well, a lot of them stemming from research conducted by forensic experts at the Federal Bureau of Investigation. Although a standardized methodology and etiquette was followed, much of it having been derived from Song Ci's ancient book indicating the timelessness of the things that were discussed in it, specific niches of forensic science began to be explored as well, with advancements in nuclear technology as well as the fields of physics and chemistry helping give these advancements little pushes here and there along the way. All in all, the twentieth century saw unbelievable progress in all aspects of forensic methodology and techniques.

This is also where forensic science began to merge in many ways with molecular biology. Although a thousand years ago, pioneers of forensic methodology such as Song Ci, as well as unwitting exponents of forensic technique such as Archimedes, could never have predicted that the fluids from a perpetrator's body could result in the apprehension of said perpetrator—such a thing only became a reality as genetic science advanced far enough to allow human beings to examine and alter the fundamental biological storage unit of our body. The advancements that such a discovery brought to the field of forensics were incalculable and, in many ways, highly unexpected.

The true pioneers of DNA-based forensic analysis were several pathologists that lived during the twentieth century. A few of these pathologists are Francis Camps, Sydney Smith, and Keith Simpson. These pathologists, as well as several other scientists that were pivotal to the development of forensic techniques and methodology, will be discussed in detail in the next chapter, with detailed accounts of their accomplishments and the progress each of them made in an individual capacity in the field of forensics. Their contributions to forensic science were pivotal to the formation of the modern day forensic methodology.

Influential Figures in Forensic Science

There are a number of people that have been pivotal to the improvement and advancement of forensic science, especially in the twentieth century. In this century, a scientific discipline that had been perpetually nascent for a very long time had finally made it to the limelight, and several proponents of this field brought their heads together and made progress in leaps and bounds.

There are far too many influential scientists in this field to create a complete list; however the following are some of those who made a significant contribution in forensic science and methodology.

Francis Edward Camps

Francis Edward Camps[xxii] is one of the pathologists responsible for the furthering of forensic science in the twentieth century. Born in the small town of Teddington in the English county of Middlesex to a surgeon and general practitioner by the name of Percy William Leopold, Camps underwent a high-class education, which facilitated his later rise as a pathologist, providing him with a broad and creative mind that later helped him apply the various aspects of his branch of science within the realm of forensic science.

Camps began his education at the prestigious prep school called Marlborough. He moved on to higher education at Guy's Hospital, where he studied to become a doctor like his father. After completing his postgraduate education at the Liverpool School of Topical Medicine and the Neuchatel University in Switzerland, Camps decided to specialize in the medical field of pathology, gaining employment at the Chelmsford and Essex Hospital. As the field of forensic science began to grow to encompass fields of medicine such as pathology, he gained interest in the criminal justice procedure as well, becoming involved with several landmark cases in the history of forensic science during his lifetime.

The majority of the cases he provided testimony for were cases of alcohol poisoning, allowing him to make some major advancements in the field of toxicology. These cases were mostly suicides, but perhaps the most important case that Camps was involved in was of a nature far more sinister.

The case in question was that of serial murderer John Christie. Camps performed autopsies on the bodies of the victims that were found at the scene of the crime, providing detailed reports that helped authorities work out Christie's modus operandi due to the consistent methods he used in his murders. This helped forensic pathology gain some serious credibility in the criminal investigative system. It also helped posthumously exonerate an innocent man that had been falsely convicted of the crime and executed for it, eventually leading to the abolishment of capital punishment in the United Kingdom.

Sydney Smith

Sir Sydney Alfred Smith[xxiii] was an extremely influential forensic scientist who also originated as a pathologist before eventually moving into criminology as a medico-legal advisor. Born in a small town in New Zealand, Smith's educational background is especially diverse, with him having studied technical biological fields such as botany and zoology, along with a specialization in the forensic aspect of medicine. Smith started out as a general practitioner before becoming a forensic assistant in Edinburgh. However, he was not able to hone his forensic skills for very long, as the First World War ended up interrupting his employment.

After serving in the war as a Major, Smith took up employment as a medico-legal officer for the Egyptian government while simultaneously occupying the post of senior lecturer at the School of Medicine at the University of Cairo. During this stint in Egypt, Smith greatly furthered the field of ballistics analysis, a most important field of forensic science. Indeed, during this period Smith became somewhat of an authority on ballistics analysis and firearm-related forensic science, so much so that he ended up writing the *Textbook of Forensic Medicine*, a book that is still today an important part of the forensic science curriculum around the world.

Smith was involved in several important cases during his life, cases that honed his interest in ballistic analysis. The first noteworthy case that he was involved with in a medico-legal advisory capacity was the trial of a man named Patrick Higgins for the murder of his two sons. Smith, through forensic analysis, was able to determine that the boys had been killed by being drowned in a flooded quarry, something that he deduced by noticing a build up of adipocere, also known as corpse wax, on the boys. Adipocere is formed by the decomposition of tissue in dead bodies subjected to moisture.

Smith was also an integral part of the forensic team that helped convict murderer Buck Ruxton, a case that proved to be a landmark in the field of forensic science due to the innovative forensic techniques involved. His innovative idea during this case was to identify a victim by superimposing a photograph of the victim over an x-ray of the victim's skull. Smith's ideas set the standard for forensic scientists, one of a creative yet logical thinker that was able to think outside the box to find solutions, much as Archimedes did with King Hiero's crown.

Smith eventually became a professor of forensic medicine at the University of Edinburgh and ultimately Dean of the Faculty of Medicine, where he influenced many young forensic minds. Smith received a knighthood during his later years and wrote an autobiography detailing the thought process behind his forensic methodology, a book that became immensely popular for the candid and frank way in which it discusses the importance and logic behind forensic techniques used in the criminal investigative system, thereby sealing his well-deserved place as one of the paragons of forensic science and methodology.

Keith Simpson

Cedric Keith Simpson,[xxiv] more commonly known as Keith Simpson, is another addition to the list of English doctors that specialized in pathology who eventually went on to revolutionize the fast-growing world of forensic science. A child prodigy of sorts, Simpson had started teaching pathology at Guy's Hospital when he was only twenty-five, something that indicates the strength of the intellect that would go on to so greatly influence so many different fields of forensic science. He held that post two years before making his first foray into medical criminology and forensic science.

At the age of twenty-seven, Simpson received a promotion of sorts and began supervising postmortems and autopsies that were conducted at Guy's Hospital. His effectiveness in this department was so great that only four years later he became the official medico-legal advisor to the police constabulary that held jurisdiction in the county of Surrey, a position that he would use to help solve a string of cases. He eventually came to be known as the leading forensic pathologist in England, helping to truly define the term and all the duties that such a job entailed, setting the standard for the practices that future forensic pathologists would follow.

In 1947, about ten years after Simpson became the medico-legal advisor for the police constabulary that held jurisdiction in Surrey, he published a book called *Simpson's Forensic Medicine*, which is now considered a staple of forensic education in universities that teach the subject around the world. Three years after this seminal volume of forensic methodology was published, Simpson collaborated with other major forensic pathologists, including Francis Camps and Sydney Smith, who were described in earlier chapters, for what can arguably be called the single greatest achievement of his life.

This achievement was the creation of the Association of Forensic Medicine, of which he was the first ever President as well, in the year 1950. This resulted in the creation of a forum where forensic scientists could come together and discuss and debate ways to improve their craft, allowing the field of forensic science to improve by leaps and bounds.

Simpson had the impressive distinction of having performed more autopsies than any other pathologist in the world. This meant that he performed postmortems on some very famous cases specifically assigned to him because of his reputation as a forensic pathologist.

One of the most important cases that Simpson was involved in was the infamous case of John George Haigh, who attempted to dispose of his victims' bodies by using acid. Smith, through his brilliance as a forensic pathologist, was able to determine that Haigh had been using acid to dispose of the bodies of his victims. He found this out by closely examining the sludge found in Haigh's workshop and discovering gallstones and a pair of dentures, which was sufficient forensic evidence to allow the court to convict and execute the man.

Alec Jeffreys

All of the previous people mentioned in this section were pathologists that applied their discipline in a forensic context, thereby giving birth to new innovations that helped improve and broaden the scope of forensic science. Alec Jeffreys[xxv] is not a pathologist, but he applied the same philosophy as his fellows in this section.

Born in 1950, Alec Jeffreys is a genetic scientist and one of the most important figures in the field of forensic science because he applied his knowledge of genetics and DNA to forensic methodology to give birth to one of the most important and well-known fields of forensic science: DNA profiling.

To apply pathology to forensic methodology was not much of an innovation in and of itself. The very nature of forensics meant that trace evidence on and inside of bodies would be pivotal to the solving of cases. However, no one had really imagined that a thing such as DNA could ever be used in a forensic context until Jeffreys came along and completely revolutionized the field of forensic science by creating what can now arguably be called its single most important and effective branch.

Jeffreys's invention of DNA profiling began in a way that evoked the man that first applied forensic methodology so many millennia ago, the philosopher previously discussed, Archimedes. What this means is that Jeffreys, whilst examining the results of a DNA experiment, had a 'eureka' moment much like the ancient Greek philosopher. The DNA he was examining was that of his technician as well as members of the technician's family, and while he was analyzing it he began to notice the similarities and differences between the DNA of these people that were so closely related to each other. In less than an hour, Jeffreys knew the scope of using people's unique genetic code, something that is even more unique than one's fingerprint.

DNA fingerprinting, as it is now called, has become an absolutely essential part of the criminal investigative process. Although initially used to settle immigration and paternity disputes, soon those involved in the criminal investigative process saw the potential of this innovation and began to use it to solve murders.

The very first person that was apprehended and convicted with the help of DNA fingerprinting was a murderer and rapist by the name of Colin Pitchfork. This was done by matching the semen found in the two girls he had raped and killed with a sample of his DNA. Now, DNA fingerprinting is the single most effective way of proving that a suspect was at the scene of a crime. The technique has greatly improved upon the number of criminals that are correctly convicted as well as reduced the number of falsely accused innocent people who are convicted of a crime that they did not commit. Such is the significance of this innovation that it is going to be discussed in detail in the next chapter of this book.

Joseph Bell

Out of all of the figures in history that have made an impact on forensic science, perhaps none have been more significant than a man by the name of Joseph Bell.[xxvi] The great grandson of a forensic surgeon, one can go so far as to say that forensic science had always been in Bell's blood. Although he was not involved in as many cases as some of his contemporaries in this section of the book, nor did he make any singularly significant innovations in the field of forensic science, Bell is still one of the most important people in the history of forensic science simply because he helped shape the mindset of the modern day forensic analyst.

A very interesting fact to note about Joseph Bell is that while he worked at the Edinburgh Royal Infirmary, a man who served as his clerk was inspired by him so much that he ended up writing books about a character based on him, which eventually became one of the most popular book series in the world. This clerk was named Arthur Conan Doyle, and the character he created is a detective we have already discussed earlier, a man who goes by the singularly recognizable name of Sherlock Holmes. This helps give one an inkling of the kind of man that Bell was, as many of Sherlock Holmes's almost superhuman powers of deduction are inspired by a real man that helped shape the field of forensic science.

Bell's influence stems entirely from the fact that he taught forensic science to so many students while he was a professor at the University of Edinburgh and was so pivotal in moulding the way that they would approach forensic science. Since he taught forensic science in the first half of the nineteenth century, it was his students that would go on to make innovations in the field of forensic science after its popularization. Bell's single most important suggestion to his students was his consistent emphasis on the importance of close observation during analysis before making a diagnosis. In order to describe to his students what kind of close observation was required, Bell would pick random strangers and deduce many things about that stranger, such as where they worked or what they had recently been doing. This is very interesting to note because this is one of Sherlock Holmes's most famous abilities.

Bell's powers of deduction made him a pioneer of sorts in the field of forensic science and forensic pathology, a field that would end up influencing the direction of forensic science for the first half of the twentieth century, and which arguably led to the creation of DNA profiling. Many of the forensic pathologists that have been mentioned in this section, such as Francis Camp and Sydney Smith, can be said to have been students of Bell even if they never studied under him, simply because he was so far ahead of his time with a grasp of forensic methodology that seemed almost instinctive in a time where practically no one in the world took forensic science all that seriously yet.

Alphonse Bertillon

Alphonse Bertillon[xxvii] has been mentioned before, but here his various accomplishments and innovations shall be discussed in detail. Many years ahead of his time, the fact that many of Bertillon's innovations were eventually rendered obsolete by more advanced forensic techniques does not take into account the fact that the vast majority of these techniques were invented in the first place because they had the platform of Bertillon's original ideas to expand on. In this way, Bertillon's various innovations were absolutely pivotal to the field of forensic science, and the fact that he was an innovator in this field almost a century before any real interest was shown in it is singularly impressive as well.

Bertillon's most famous innovation was anthropometry, a system of criminal profiling based on the measurements of a criminal, which provided police with details about said criminal's body proportions. Because criminals could only be identified by name or photograph before this innovation, it can be argued that Bertillon invented the whole concept of profiling in the first place, of a system whereby a criminal could be identified regardless of their appearance or any low-level trickery on their part. In this manner, Bertillon was influential in the creation of one of the most basic areas of forensic science. Simply put, if those that came after him invented the car, Bertillon was the man that invented the wheel, as he was responsible for the creation of all of the most basic aspects of forensic science.

Photography of criminals had become somewhat common ever since the invention of photography, but the photos were often taken in a haphazard way. Bertillon, on the other hand, was the man that saw the merits of this procedure and standardized the whole process. This standardization of the process of photographing criminals led to one of his most important innovations out of the many that he made over the course of his illustrious career. This innovation was called the mug shot. A mug shot is a picture of a convicted felon in front of a plain background in front and side poses. This was to facilitate the possession of visual records of what criminals look like in order to aid in their capture if they escape from prison and to help warn people of their presence. The importance of this innovation can be seen by the fact that mug shots are still taken in today's modern day and age; such is the universality and timelessness of Bertillon's invention.

Bertillon applied forensic methodology to practically every aspect of the criminal investigative process. He introduced a logical way of approaching crime solving in a time where most criminal investigations were ad hoc and haphazard. It is fair to say that without Bertillon and his innovative forensic techniques, forensic science as we know it today would certainly not exist.

Wilfrid Derome

Wilfrid Derome[xxviii] has the singular distinction of breaking the European monopoly of this list of influential figures in the history of forensic science, as he is Canadian. After studying the arts, Derome became a doctor and specialized in toxicology after gaining an interest in that particular branch of forensic science. Derome eventually taught legal medicine and toxicology, essentially a general subject comprising forensic methodology, at the University of Montreal. He was very influential to his students, many of which would go on to become innovative forensic scientists themselves and would contribute to Canada becoming one of the countries with the most influential forensic scientists in the late twentieth century.

Derome's single greatest achievement was the building of the very first forensic lab in North America. Forensic science had, for the longest time, been a discipline practiced mostly in Europe with very little innovation being made in North America. Derome became the biggest reason that changed after he built

North America's first forensic laboratory. J. Edgar Hoover, the founder of the Federal Bureau of Investigation, eventually visited this laboratory before building a forensic library for the Bureau in the United States of America.

Derome's main contributions to the field of forensic science were his innovations in the specific fields of toxicology and ballistic analysis. He became the first person in North America to provide testimony in court based on forensic analysis and provide evidence derived from both of these fields of forensic science in said court. This set an important precedent, one that opened the floodgates and allowed forensic methodology to be taken seriously in North American courts, something that was far more common in European courtrooms.

The testimony he provided based on toxicology was the discovery of the presence of ethyl alcohol, a poisonous substance, in the blood of a recently deceased person through forensic analysis of the victim's blood. This helped prove that the person's death was the result of foul play rather than natural causes as had been previously thought.

Derome's innovation that allowed ballistic

analysis to be applied in a way that was practical and admissible in court was an invention called the microspherometer. This invention allowed forensic analysts to examine the surface of bullets and reveal the marks left on their surface by the firearm they were shot out of. The microspherometer allowed forensic analysts to match bullets to guns in a way that was logical and plain to see, and resulted in the first ever arrest in history based on ballistic analysis.

Derome is singularly important for popularizing and innovating forensic science in a part of the world that was falling behind in this field. His innovations can arguably be said to have resulted in the creation of the FBI, which took many of their forensic methods and techniques from those proposed and endorsed by Derome, as was the case with the forensic lab that they built.

Paul Leland Kirk

Paul Leland Kirk[xxix] is the first American in this section; he is also the first person discussed whose background is not in medicine or a branch of the discipline, but in chemistry. The genesis of his interest in forensic science occurred when he became a professor at the University of Berkeley when a student asked him, in a purely chemical context, if he could deduce through chemical analysis if a dog had died due to the fact that it had been poisoned. This piqued his interest somewhat, but what really got him interested in forensic science was a much more significant event.

Since Kirk was a well-known specialist in the field of microscopy, authorities approached him and asked him to examine the clothes of a rape victim for trace evidence. Kirk was successfully able to find fibres on the victim's clothing that matched the fibres of the shirt that her attacker had worn during the incident. This ended up getting the rapist convicted. After seeing the good he could do with his knowledge, the people that he could potentially help, Kirk made the decision to enter into the field of forensic chemical analysis permanently with the hopes of making a positive impact on the world.

Kirk eventually became the leader of his university's criminology program, creating the technical criminology major and eventually becoming the chairperson of the criminalistics department. Kirk's innovative use of close analysis of trace evidence ended up having a great impact on the way that crime scene integrity was seen, as he felt that even the smallest piece of evidence could potentially lead to a conviction. He became a key figure in the creation of one of the most important and specific branches of forensic science, that of blood spatter analysis, which is now used to great effect to help paint a picture of how a murder was committed.

This innovation regarding blood spatter analysis came about as the result of him being asked to examine the evidence in the case of Sam Shepard, a man accused and convicted of murdering his wife. Upon examining the photographs and visiting the crime scene, he noticed odd details about the way the blood had spattered against the wall. Kirk came to the conclusion that Shepard had not murdered his wife, as the way the blood would have been spilled would have been very different had that been the case.

After a decade of unsuccessful appeals and motions, a decade that Shepard spent in jail for a murder that he had not committed, the court finally looked at the evidence Kirk was offering and acquitted him of his crimes, leaving him free to go. Kirk's innovative use of forensic methodology led to the creation of blood spatter analysis as a proper field of forensic analysis.

Alexandre Lacassagne

Alexandre Lacassagne[xxx] is an influential figure in the history of forensic science as well as the history of criminology as a whole. His ideas about crime and how it should be solved, and indeed how perpetrators of crime should be punished, were hugely influential in shaping the way the modern world approached the subject of criminology, laying the foundation for many of the concepts and ideas that we possess and implement today. Lacassagne possessed a large amount of interest in the fields of sociology and psychology as well as criminology, which led to the development of what came to be known as the Lacassagne school of criminology.

At the time, the general consensus among the public was that a criminal was born evil in some way, mostly in the lower classes, and it was just a matter of time before such people ended up committing a crime. Lacassagne disagreed with this concept completely, asserting that criminals were not born, but *made*, and that environmental influences were more important than genetic influences in the creation of a criminal. This view on criminals was surprisingly liberal for the time, and eventually overshadowed other more backward schools of criminology that asserted criminals were born bad in some way, that crime was in their genes.

His influence on the field of forensic science is immense. He specialized in the field of toxicology and was the first person to propose that there might be a way to determine whether a person had been poisoned or not by examining their blood, although he was unable to successfully invent a way to do this. He was also one of the earliest proponents of blood spatter analysis, believing that the way that blood fell said a lot about the way that a crime had played out. His thoughts on blood spatter analysis were what ended up inspiring Paul Leland Kirk's examination of the scene of the murder of Sam Shepard's wife.

Lacassagne was also pivotal in the field of ballistics analysis. He was the first person to notice the markings on a bullet and to propose that there might be a way to connect a bullet that had been fired to the gun it had been fired from as a way to determine the identity of the shooter. Although he was once again unable to devise a method to apply his concept, the idea that he had is what eventually inspired Wilfrid Derome to create his device that fulfilled this very purpose.

Although Lacassagne did not invent anything of note during his lifetime, he did lay down the blueprints for several important innovations in the field of forensic science that would occur in the years to come by people inspired by his ideas and concepts. He is similar to Bertillon in this way, an innovator without whom many of the most important aspects of forensic methodology would have been greatly delayed or might even have never been discovered at all.

Edmond Locard

One would be hard pressed to find a personality in the world of forensic science as singularly influential as Edmond Locard.[xxxi] His name is synonymous with forensic science, simply because so many of his innovations are what ended up shaping the way forensic techniques would be applied in the criminal investigative process. In many ways, Locard is similar to Joseph Bell in that his powers of deduction were what inspired many of his students to enter the field of forensic science and make innovations of their own in the century that contained the most forensic innovations in history. It is interesting to note, following this comparison of Locard to a man that ended up inspiring the creation of Sherlock Holmes, that he was called 'the Sherlock Holmes of France' due to his deductive prowess and instinctive knowledge of forensic science.

However, unlike Bell, whose significance stems solely from how much he influenced his students with his deductive powers rather than any innovations or inventions on his part, Locard made a lot of innovations in the field of forensic science as well. His contributions to the field of forensic science, apart from the students that he inspired, are vast, but two of them stand out as major contributions that he deserves to be praised for.

The first of these two was the creation of a concept that came to be known as "Locard's exchange principle." This principle states that the perpetrator of the crime is definitely going to bring something to the scene of his or her crime that they will leave behind that can later be discovered and used as evidence. The gist of this principle can be summed up in the following phrase: every contact leaves a trace. This basically means that crime scenes are bound to have some sort of trace evidence that can tie the perpetrator of the crime to the scene of the crime, and if such evidence is not found, it is not because the perpetrator failed to leave it, it is because the investigators failed to find it.

Locard's second major contribution to the field of forensic science occurred in the year 1910. Before this time, Locard had served as the assistant to Alexandre Lacassagne, who influenced much of his work. After leaving his job with Lacassagne, Locard was able to procure funds from the police department of Lyon in France to secure two rooms and two assistants. These two rooms are what became the world's very first police laboratory, a space specifically designed for the purpose of forensic analysis, and thus Locard's second great contribution to the world of forensic analysis.

This was the first time in history that such a space had been developed, that forensic analysis was seen as something so delicate and subtle that a controlled environment was required in order to perform said analysis successfully. Hence, the creation of this forensic laboratory is one of the most pivotal moments in the history of forensic science as a discipline.

Albert Sherman Osborn

Albert Sherman Osborn,[xxxii] one of the founding members of the FBI, along with J. Edgar Hoover, is a significant figure in the history of forensics because he is largely responsible for a very important, though often overlooked, branch of forensic analysis. This forensic analysis involves the examination of documents provided in court suspected to be fake or forged and determining their legitimacy.

This process, called questioned document analysis, involves, first and foremost, establishment of the genuineness, or lack thereof, of the document in question, as well as revealing any alterations or additions that have been made to the original draft of the document. If the document has been composed by hand, questioned document analysis involves ascertaining the source of the handwriting as well as the true author of the document, if such a thing is disputed by the court. If the document has been composed via a typewriter or a computer, questioned document analysis involves ascertaining the source of the document, as well as the source of any and all marks and impressions that have been left upon said document.

By creating this very specific branch of forensic science, Osborn paved a way for the courts to demand legitimate documents. Before Osborn, illegitimate documents were impossible to detect, as there was simply no system in place to weed out the forgeries, fakes, and altered documents. Thanks to his questioned document analysis, many white-collar criminals responsible for embezzlement and other money-related crimes have been put behind bars.

Questioned document analysis has now become one of the most important forensic sciences available because of the huge amounts of money that are in play in the world today. With Ponzi schemes a perpetual danger and embezzlers infesting virtually every company making big money, this branch of forensic science never seems to get the attention nor the respect it deserves. It is responsible for keeping greedy people from plundering pension funds and company profits, helping keep the world's economy in balance.

Archibald Reiss

Archibald Reiss,[xxxiii] born in Germany in the late nineteenth century, is singularly important to the history of forensic science because of his contributions to the proliferation of the teaching of forensic methodology. Receiving a Ph. D. in chemistry at the incredibly young age of twenty-two, Reiss had a natural aptitude for forensic science and photography. This allowed him to expand on Bertillon's standardization of photography in the criminal investigative process and improve the way that mug shots were taken, taking into account the height of the person being photographed as well. His innovations regarding photography in the criminal investigative process were recorded and published in a book called *Forensic Photography*. The techniques mentioned in the book laid the groundwork for how modern day crime scene photos are taken.

He eventually became a professor of forensic science at his alma mater, the University of Lausanne in Switzerland. Once in this position, Reiss quickly began instituting programs de-

signed specifically to teach students about forensic science and, in 1909, inaugurated the
Institute of Forensic Science at his university.
This institute was one of the first institutes in
the world dedicated to the teaching of forensic
methodology and its various subtypes, not to
mention one of the first of its kind that was
opened at a university as well regarded as the
University of Lausanne.

Reiss published two more works that detailed his opinions on forensic technique,
books that are still taught from at the University of Lausanne today. When the First World
War broke out, Reiss was unable to continue
his forensic research and education. After the
war was over, he established a police academy in Serbia, the country he had decided to
settle down in, where he continued teaching
forensic science until his death.

Reiss's creation of one of the first institu-
tions within a university that offered programs
specifically related to forensic science was in-
calculably important in making people take the
discipline seriously. His innovations and opinions involving forensic science, particularly in
the fields of toxicology and forensic photog-

raphy, a field often undervalued, helped to shape the way forensic analysts approached their work for many decades into the future.

One aspect of his influence that was particularly important was the enthusiasm with which he taught. To him, forensic science was not just a means to an end; it was a puzzle that was meant to be solved, a way to get to the bottom of all of life's mysteries. The wonder that he instilled in his students is probably what ended up inspiring so many of them to make innovations of their own in the field of forensic science.

Bernard Spilsbury

Sir Bernard Henry Spilsbury[xxxiv] is yet another addition to the almost endless list of pathologists who majorly affected the field of forensic science during the twentieth century. He was one of the most prolific forensic pathologists in the world, with his cases encompassing not just postmortem examinations and autopsies, but toxicology reports as well. Indeed, Spilsbury might be one of the biggest reasons that toxicology is taken as seriously as it is these days, simply because he was one of the first people to use this branch of forensic science, and he used it to obtain great results.

Having specialized in the nascent branch of medicine known as forensic pathology, Spilsbury first came into the public eye when he successfully identified the unidentifiable remains of a human body by analyzing a piece of scar tissue. Another famous case that Spilsbury gave testimony for was one of the first cases in which he provided evidence following a toxicology exam, the case of Herbert

Rowse Armstrong, who was accused of killing his wife. After analyzing the blood of the victim, Spilsbury was able to prove that the cause of death was poisoning via arsenic, due to a high presence of the chemical in her body.

However, the case that made him a virtual celebrity in terms of being a forensic pathologist was entirely different. The case was known in the media as the "Brides in the Bath" case. The case involved three women who had died in their bathtubs seemingly by accident. When a man by the name George Joseph Smith was brought in as a suspect in one of the deaths, Spilsbury was able to prove that he was the perpetrator through his testimony. He claimed that goose bumps on the victim's skin at the time of her death and the fact she was found clutching a bar of soap not only proved that she was afraid when she had died, but she had also died a violent death. Through further examination of forensic evidence, the authorities were able to convict Smith of all three murders.

The unique and inventive methods that Spilsbury used to solve the mystery led him to be hailed as the best forensic pathologist in

England. Spilsbury solved a number of cases in his lifetime, all of which were influential in setting precedents that future judges would use to treat forensic evidence more favourably than they would have otherwise.

Auguste Ambroise Tardieu

Auguste Ambroise Tardieu[xxxv] lived in the latter half of the nineteenth century, and his innovative ideas and approach to forensic science and methodology made him quite possibly the single most important forensic scientist of that era. Specializing in toxicology and setting the stage for many of the innovations that would be brought about by the next generation of forensic scientists, Tardieu had a long and illustrious career, spanning twenty-three years in which he made a reputation for himself that was well deserved, owing to the man's dedication and unparalleled work ethic.

Over the course of his decades-long career, Tardieu participated as a forensic analyst in well over 5,000 cases. He maintained meticulous records of the cases he participated in and constantly examined the particulars of old cases hoping to see them from a new angle and spot something that he had missed the first time around. This method of record keeping allowed him to learn from his own spontaneity and inspired the meticulous way in which forensic evidence and reports are kept in to-day's criminal investigative process as well.

His vast records allowed him to become possibly one of the most prolific authors of texts about forensic science in history. Tardieu published dozens of books, not just about fo-rensic science, but about statistics he had not-ed regarding abortions, suicides, homosexuali-ty, insanity, and other such aspects of human society. His records also allowed him to make some important innovations in the field of fo-rensic science, innovations stemming from a particular passion of pursuing those who harmed children. A lot of Tardieu's published works are about violence against children, which led him to discover a unique feature of newborn babies that had been strangled.

Tardieu found that infants who had been killed in this manner had bruising caused by ruptured blood vessels inside their lungs. Be-fore this discovery, it was relatively easy for perpetrators to kill babies in this manner and get away with it, but after Tardieu made his findings public, authorities were able to catch people that would do this sort of thing.

These spots are referred to as Tardieu's

ecchymoses, and this discovery is probably reason enough to call him one of the greatest forensic scientists of the nineteenth century, if not of all time.

Paul Theodore Uhlenhuth

Paul Theodor Uhlenhuth[xxxvi] is the only true microbiologist in this section. Rather than pathology or chemistry, specializations that, as you have probably noticed, give birth to many of the world's forensic scientists, Uhlenhuth specialized in bacteriology and immunology. Although these specializations may seem widely different from anything forensic science would be about, keep in mind that genetic science doesn't seem to have much to do with forensic science at first glance either, yet it gave birth to one of the most revolutionary fields of forensic science in the history of the field. Uhlenhuth is a surprising addition to this list, but an important one all the same.

Although Uhlenhuth would not be considered a forensic scientist by any means, he did make one contribution to the field of forensic analysis that completely revolutionized the criminal justice system in the twentieth century. This contribution was the creation of the precipitin test, a test that would enable one to tell if a sample of blood had been derived from an animal or from a human being. Although Uhlenhuth had not intended to apply this test in a criminological setting, those involved in the criminal investigative process hailed the test as a dream come true.

Before this test became a reality, people suspected of a murder that were found with blood on their clothing could claim that it had come from an animal and it would be extremely difficult to prove that they were lying, and absolutely impossible to prove this if there were no witnesses on hand to provide testimony to the contrary. However, with this test, all that had to be done to find out whether the suspect's alibi was true or not was to conduct this forensic exam, which would reveal whether the blood was from a human being or from an animal.

An example of the usefulness of this test in a criminological setting is in the case of two children that had been dismembered in the town of Gohren. The prime suspect in this case had been found with what looked like blood on his clothes. However, he claimed that it was simply a wood stain from a carpentry project that he had been undertaking. Since there were no witnesses to prove he was lying, if the test had not been invented yet, the authorities would have had no choice but to let the suspect go. However, the test revealed the rust-coloured stains on the man's clothes were actually dried human blood, which allowed authorities to arrest and convict him for murdering two innocent children in cold blood.

DNA Profiling and Other Branches of Forensic Science

As forensic science went from being in a state of perpetual nascence to a fast advancing discipline, many different subtypes of the field began to develop with their own distinct flavours, but all of which fell under the general umbrella of forensic science and methodology. Out of all of the branches of forensic science that had come about in the twentieth century, by far the most innovative and most successful is DNA profiling, also known as DNA fingerprinting.[xxxvii]

The incredible accuracy with which trace DNA found at a crime scene can be matched with a DNA sample acquired from a suspect makes it the best way to keep track of criminals and create their profiles, apart from perhaps fingerprint analysis and comparison, which could arguably come in at a close second.

As has been mentioned in the previous chapter, a man named Alec Jeffreys discovered DNA profiling in an accidental 'eureka' moment while he was examining DNA samples of a lab technician and the technician's relatives. The accuracy of the results of a DNA test occurs despite the fact that most humans share 99.9% of DNA with each other. This is because the miniscule portion of DNA that does differ from person to person is unique enough to distinguish between two different individuals. However, in cases where monozygotic twins, or identical twins, are concerned, the accuracy of a DNA test drops considerably. This is because monozygotic twins share a lot more of their DNA with each other than fraternal twins or other siblings.

The process of DNA analysis is fairly complicated. Obviously a DNA sample needs to have been obtained from the crime scene in order to have something with which compare the DNA of the suspect. If DNA has been recovered from the crime scene and a suspect has been apprehended, a DNA sample from the suspect is now required. There are several ways to obtain a DNA sample from a suspect, some of which are more effective than others.

Buccal swabs[xxxviii] are usually considered the best way to get DNA samples from suspects. A buccal swab essentially involves taking a cotton bud and rubbing it against the inside of a suspect's cheek. This is the most popular way to collect sample DNA from a suspect for several reasons. First and foremost, the DNA collected has the least chance of undergoing contamination if this technique is used to collect it. Secondly, the procedure is noninvasive, and it is always better to collect DNA in a noninvasive manner in case the person is innocent. Using invasive procedures on suspects that are guilty may allow them to unnecessarily escape justice citing an abuse of power on the officer of authority's part.

If collecting DNA via a buccal swab is not an option, there are other ways in which a sample of the suspect's DNA can be obtained. DNA samples can be collected from a suspect's toothbrush or razor, basically any common item that the suspect uses that has a good chance of collecting saliva, blood, sperm or any other kind of tissue or fluid that contains DNA. If such an item cannot be obtained for whatever reason, there is one other way to collect a sample of the suspect's DNA. This involves obtaining DNA from a stored sample of the suspect's tissue if it is available—for example, samples of sperm that have been stored at a sperm bank, blood from a blood bank, or biopsy tissue.

If none of the aforementioned methods for collecting DNA are available, a final option is available, but it is highly unreliable. This involves collecting the DNA sample from a relative of the suspect. This can provide an indication of sorts if a match is on the cards. Since this method is not very reliable, forensic analysts only use it as a last resort when they are out of options. The sample taken must be from a blood relative of the suspect, that is to say a relative by birth, and not by marriage or law.

Once a sample of the DNA of the suspect has been collected, it is analyzed and compared to the DNA found at the crime scene. There are several different ways to analyze and compare the two DNA samples, each of which has its own benefits and flaws. Three of the various methods that forensic analysts use to compare different samples of DNA, along with details regarding their process and what pros and cons there are to using each of them, are all included in the following list:

1) **RFLP Analysis.**[xxxix] This method involves firstly collecting the DNA from the cells obtained from the suspect and then breaking it down into small pieces by using a restriction enzyme. Once this procedure has been performed, the thousands of fragments that are obtained vary in size depending on differences between the various sequences of genes that are present in the body of the person from whom the sample originated. A technique called gel electrophoresis is then used to separate the bits of DNA based on their size, after which they are placed on a filter made of either nitrocellulose or nylon, in a procedure referred to as the Southern blot. This results in the pieces of DNA becoming attached to the filter and the DNA strands becoming denatured. Probe molecules that have been radiolabeled are then used to ensure that only unique DNA fragments are left present on the filter, with the repeated fragments binding themselves to the molecule, after which the filter is examined under an x-ray. The process is repeated with the other

sample and the results are compared. This method requires a lot of effort, as you can see from its description, and demands a large amount of pristine DNA. As a result, it is not very popular these days.

2) **Y-Chromosome Analysis.**[xl] Since Y chromosomes are paternally inherited, this test also works with DNA obtained from a paternal relative of the suspect, something that greatly improves its usefulness. However, this technique is useless when applied to a DNA sample provided by a woman or from a maternal relative of the suspect. Additionally, the results obtained are weaker than those obtained using autosomal chromosome analysis, which is a more popular method of DNA analysis.

3) **Mitochondrial Analysis.**[xli] This method of DNA analysis works surprisingly well with highly degraded DNA samples, which is one aspect of this test that gives it an edge over the various other methods of DNA analysis. Mitochondrial DNA, which is the type of DNA that is

required in order to conduct this form of DNA analysis, can be obtained from hair shafts, as well as calcium deposits in aged bones and teeth. A famous example of the use of mitochondrial analysis is when a woman approached the Russian royal family and claimed to be the long lost princess, Anastasia. She was proved to be a fraud when an mtDNA sample from her failed to match a sample that the royal family still possessed of Anastasia.

As in all method of forensic analysis, there are certain problems that occur during DNA analysis.[xlii] DNA-based evidence provided in courts is still sometimes referred to as spurious when the match provided allows for twelve other people that possess the same DNA sequence. This has resulted in several severe miscarriages of justice due to the fact that DNA analysis technology is not advanced enough to accurately assess samples that have undergone moderate degradation, something that can be very difficult to prevent. It is also, at times, difficult to obtain DNA samples that have maintained their integrity, as it is very possible that a suspect cannot be located in order to obtain a DNA sample. In these cases, when the aforementioned alternate methods are used, such as the acquiring of DNA from a toothbrush or biopsy tissue, many times the DNA has already been degraded before the forensic analysts collected it. Even if the DNA is pristine, it is possible that two separate samples of DNA can be obtained from a toothbrush, which can occur during contamination of collection of the sample, or during the test itself.

DNA obtained from a stored sample of tissue also often causes problems, as the results of analysis on such samples is often not as accurate nor as conclusive as tests and analyses conducted on fresh DNA collected straight from the source via buccal swab. All in all, it is plain to see how, despite its accuracy under ideal conditions, DNA analysis still has a long way to go before it becomes the kind of forensic tool that can provide results in which there is absolutely no chance of doubt.

There is also the fact that DNA analysis has been around for so long, criminals have started wising up to the ways that they can get caught using this forensic technique. Many criminals have started using false DNA as a way to fake their way out of a DNA analysis. In other situations, people end up getting framed for crimes that they didn't commit because the true perpetrator planted their DNA at the scene of the crime.

A poignant example of how criminals are starting to account for DNA analysis in their attempts to escape justice can be seen in the case of John Schneeberger, a South African doctor who practiced medicine in Canada in the 1990s. One night, Schneeberger[xliii] took advantage of the fact that his female patient was sedated and raped her. Unfortunately for him, his patient remembered the rape and reported him to the authorities. He had left semen on her underwear, which, one might assume, would have gotten him convicted in no time. However, police collected blood samples from him on three occasions, and on all three occasions, the DNA comparison with the semen came back negative. As it turned out, Schneeberger had surgically inserted into his arm a Penrose drain[xliv] filled with blood that was not his own as well as anticoagulants to further degrade the DNA contained within the sample. He was eventually convicted and served four years in prison before being released on parole and deported to South Africa in 2004.

DNA analysis is also reliant on the type of material that is used to collect the DNA. In general, cotton swabs are used to collect DNA, but this can backfire too. An example of such a situation is during a peculiar case where police officers in France, Germany and Austria, three countries that possess considerable distance between them, all found the presence of the same DNA at wildly different crime scenes, from murders to robberies to burglaries. There seemed to be absolutely no pattern to the way this criminal was behaving; it seemed as though he was able to be in two places at once sometimes. A sudden twist in the case occurred when the DNA sample of this master criminal matched that of a burned asylum seeker in France, and the officers began to suspect that the DNA evidence was not being all that reliable in this situation. As it turned out, the cotton swabs that they had been using were sterile but not free of DNA. The DNA that they had been profiling had come from one of the factory workers of the Australian company that manufactured these cotton swabs.

Such are the caveats that come with progress. Despite this, however, the benefits to using DNA analysis outweigh the disadvantages.

Facts About Forensic Science

Forensic science has been so successful in its improvement of the criminal justice system, and its revolution has become quite pervasive in popular culture as well. Due to the mysterious and almost magical manner in which it is used to solve crimes, the use of forensic science to catch criminals has become a popular premise for several fictional narratives. Starting with Sherlock Holmes, the book series that popularized forensic science as we know it and brought it into the public eye, there were many other examples in pop culture, even today.

The Ripper murders and the sensationalism around them also spurred forensic analysis to new heights with the publicity it received. Nowadays, forensic analysis is heavily referred to in a wide variety of shows, from *CSI* to *Criminal Minds* to *Law and Order*. The entire subgenre of television programming referred to as the police procedural features forensic science heavily, leading members of the public to make some pretty strong assumptions regarding the discipline.

However, if you were to examine the facts surrounding forensic science, you would come across a different story than the one that is presented on TV. The following facts[xlv] may surprise you about forensic science.

> The progenitors of forensic science were not, in fact, scientists! Despite the fact that forensic methodology and science, indeed forensic analysis as a whole, falls well within the confines of a scientific discipline, it might also have the singular distinction of being one of the only scientific disciplines not created by scientists. Rather, it was invented by those who would eventually find the most use for it: police officers. Indeed, it was the police officer that ended up laying the groundwork for what would eventually come to be known as forensic science and forensic methodology! It was police officers like Bertillon that helped mould the concept of what forensic science was, police officers that began to emphasize on close examina-

tion of crime scenes, on the preservation of said crime scenes due to the presence of subtle and minute trace evidence that would be lost if one was not careful but, if preserved, could result in a major breakthrough in an otherwise dead case. While it is true that certain advancements made in the twentieth century regarding forensic science were made by scientists, such as the development of DNA analysis, these advancements were made possible by the basic structure of the science laid down by the hard-working police officers that sought to change the way criminals were apprehended.

➢ It may be surprising enough to find out that scientists did not create forensic science, but that just scratches the surface of surprising facts regarding forensic science. The word *forensic* comes from Latin and means "before a forum." This term originates from one of the first uses of forensic methodology to solve a crime, after, of course, Archimedes gave

161

birth to the concept of out-of-the-box thinking within the realm of criminal investigative procedure. This instance of forensic analysis occurred around forty-four years before the Common Era, after Julius Caesar, the Emperor of Rome and the Roman Empire, was stabbed to death by the members of the Roman senate who felt as though he was acquiring too much power, a group that included his best friend Brutus. After the deed was done, the court called upon a physician by the name of Antistius to examine the body to determine who was responsible for the crime. The physician obliged and examined Caesar's body and was soon able to determine that the perpetrators were a group of senators. He named them in front of an open forum, this forum being the court, which led to the origin of the name of forensic science. This shows that forensic science has been present as a concept for millennia, along with the importance of professional doctors in the criminal investigative process.

➤ Fingerprints are not the unquestionable evidence that programs on TV would have you believe. Whereas in fictional depictions of forensic analysis, the discovery of a fingerprint most often means that the perpetrator of the crime is only moments away from being captured, based on the obvious fact that fingerprints are the most unassailable, damning pieces of evidence that can possibly be found at a crime scene, this depiction is far from the truth of the matter. As any forensic scientist worth his salt would gladly tell you, fingerprint analysis is more of an imprecise science. Although it is true that each person in the world does indeed possess a fingerprint that is absolutely unique, it is the matching of fingerprints obtained from crime scenes that causes problems. This is because the patterns that make fingerprints so unique are very difficult to discern even for experts in the field. Another reason that fingerprint analysis is sometimes not all that dependable is that the fingerprints obtained at crime scenes are often incomplete or damaged in some way, making matching them with other fingerprints very difficult. Despite advances in computer technology that have allowed forensic analysts to make more successful matches than ever before, many fingerprint tests still come out inconclusive, meaning that fingerprint analysis is not quite the game changer it is portrayed to be!

> Ballistic analysis is not all that foolproof either. Analysis of bullets and projectiles from firearms is another area of forensic science that is often portrayed to be infallible and utterly dependable. Getting a match from a bullet to the serial number of a gun often means that the perpetrator of the crime is done for! However, as is the case with fingerprints, the fact is far removed from fiction. On television programs, the boring details of ballistics analysis, fingerprint analysis, and indeed any other form of forensic analysis have to be glossed over in an effort to keep the program entertaining and to facilitate the speedy resolution of plots.

However, in real life where real forensic science is used, matching bullets and projectiles from the firearms they were launched from involves many of the same problems as fingerprint analysis, mainly due to the fact that the same basic principle applies. In ballistic analysis, the projectile that is being examined is analyzed to ascertain the pattern it possesses, allowing forensic scientists to match it to the firearm it was launched from. However, bullets that are found at crime scenes are often in no shape to be analyzed, as the force of their impact often destroys their grooves and distinct patterns. When you take into account the fact that ballistic analysis is more of a theory than a practical science that has a statistical formula behind it, it is not surprising to note that most ballistic analysis ends in an inconclusive result.

➢ DNA testing has actually been used to set people free. One of the biggest advantages of using DNA evidence in forensic analysis has been that many people convicted through a fingerprint found at the crime scene or through some other kind of evidence or testimony have been found to be innocent because someone else's DNA was found at the scene of the crime. Hence, the most surprising fact about DNA analysis is that, despite the fact that it is generally portrayed on TV to be the all-purpose, final piece of damning evidence that would nail the perpetrator of the crime and send him to jail, in real life the most useful way in which DNA evidence is used is in the exoneration of those people that were falsely convicted for crimes that they did not commit. As a result of the amnesty provided by DNA testing, several organizations across the world are attempting to make DNA testing compulsory for all convicts so that those that are innocent of their crimes can be set free.

➢ DNA testing is also not a hundred percent accurate. Despite the fact that DNA evidence and analysis of said evidence is extremely accurate, indeed so accurate that it brought about a veritable revolution in the world of forensic analysis, it is still not completely foolproof. Just like in fingerprint analysis and ballistics analysis, DNA analysis is subject to the same constraints as any other science. The true drawback of DNA analysis is that it is a science that requires extreme precision. Indeed, even the smallest mistake on the part of the analyst performing the tests can result in botched results. Additionally, DNA found in the form of trace evidence at crime scenes is often corrupted in one way or another, casting further doubts on the validity of the test. It should also be taken into account that the way a DNA sample is obtained for comparison with the trace evidence found at the crime scene also affects the results of the analysis. For example, if the suspect is not available for a buccal swab, one of the other methods for obtaining DNA must be used. These methods, which include obtaining samples of DNA stored by companies obtained via warrants, as well as samples obtained from relatives, would result in a considerably less accurate analysis than if a sample was obtained from the suspect directly. Even though DNA analysis can be extremely accurate, it is by no means foolproof.

➢ Surprisingly, one of the most accurate methods for identifying corpses is not DNA analysis or fingerprint analysis—it is dental records. For all of their benefits, DNA and fingerprint analyses are far from a hundred percent accurate as has been described in the aforementioned points, and although dental records cannot boast to be foolproof and unassailable, their accuracy rate of 93 percent is still extremely high, higher than both fingerprint analysis and DNA analysis. This is because teeth are very strong; indeed, the enamel that forms the outermost layer of teeth is the strongest material in the body, stronger even than bones, despite popular opinion believing in the opposite. DNA and fingerprints, one the other hand, are often subject to decay, as both involve obtaining a match on organic matter that decomposes over time. Teeth, however, decompose over a much longer period of time, which allows analysts to identify corpses long after their organic matter has decomposed completely. Dental records can also be used to identify victims whose bodies have been damaged beyond recognition by the manner in which they died. This makes it useful to identify victims who were killed by being burned or those who were mutilated before or after they were killed.

> It is probably clear to you by now that dental records are very important in ascertaining the identity of a victim of violence. This is not the only use for dental records in criminology! An example of dental records being used to actually convict a criminal can be seen in the case of a serial killer named Ted Bundy. Ted Bundy is possibly one of the most notorious serial killers in history, being

convicted of over thirty murders and suspected of over a hundred at the time of his execution. Bundy's modus operandi involved approaching his victims, making them feel safe due to his good looks, bludgeoning them to incapacitate them, and then strangling them. Bundy was a highly intelligent criminal who knew enough about forensic methodology to leave very little evidence at the scenes of his crimes, a fact that often surprises people, considering how brutal the crimes he committed were. As a result of his intelligence, Bundy evaded conviction of many of the crimes he had committed because police were unable to find any eyewitnesses to testify against him, nor were they able to find any forensic evidence of his presence at the scenes of the crimes. However, despite the fact that no trace evidence was found at the crime scenes that could help convict Bundy, forensic investigators noticed that one of the victims had a bite mark on her buttock. When the bite mark was compared with Bundy's, a match was found, which was enough to convict Bundy of his heinous crimes.

➢ Decomposition is a good thing! Since dental records are so accurate, more accurate than any methods of identification that rely on organic matter, most forensic analysts do not fret when a corpse is undergoing decomposition. On the contrary, they rejoice, as examining how much a body has decomposed allows forensic scientists to ascertain the time of death for the victim. This leads into another, and very creepy, fact about forensic science. Insects, although they may creep you out, would be a sight for sore eyes for any forensic scientist examining a corpse because of the information they provide. Time of death is one vital piece of information that can be discovered by examining the maggots infesting a dead body, a method that is surprisingly accurate as well. This allows investigators to ascertain when exactly the crime occurred. Studying what types of insects are present in the corpse that is being examined can also allow investigators to ascertain where the individual in question was killed.

This is because insects display endemism, which is an affinity for certain areas, something that gives investigators clues regarding the surroundings of the body at the time of death. Insects are so useful in forensic analysis that an entire field of forensic analysis has developed around their analysis, a field known as forensic entomology.

➢ One of the most important aspects of forensic science may surprise you. This aspect of forensic science relies not on precise analysis or tests conducted in sterile labs. Rather, it relies on a rather subjective part of the human body: one's sense of smell! Although a sense of smell is somewhat subjective, forensic analysts are trained to use their noses in very effective ways that can allow them to discover a lot about dead bodies. Machines are also being developed that will examine an area in which the smell of a dead body is present and discover where exactly that dead body can be found. Dead bodies emit chemicals that possess a rotten odour during decomposition. These chemicals, which include sulfur and ammonia, are what the machines being developed by forensic scientists will be searching for. Areas in which these chemicals are particularly concentrated will probably be areas in which a dead body might be found, and that is exactly where these machines will lead investigators or, if the investigators are old-school forensic analysts, they might just end up finding the dead body by the good old forensic trick of following one's nose!

➢ One's sense of smell is clearly important, as can be seen by the preceding fact. However, if you think about it, it is only logical to assume that finding dead bodies would depend a lot on your sense of smell. After all, everyone knows that dead bodies emit a strong odour, so it is easy to assume that detecting the chemicals as a way to locate a dead body would end up becoming an important part of forensic science. However, your sense of smell can also be important in uncovering the details behind another type of crime: arson. Arson is when an individual starts a fire on purpose. In cases where arson has been committed, finding out the details of the crime are absolutely essential to finding the perpetrator. These details include where the fire originated and how it was started, and one's sense of smell can be particularly useful in ascertaining the answers to both of the aforementioned questions. This is due to the fact that arsonists often use chemicals called accelerants to spread their fire over a wider area. Sniffer dogs can be used to determine if such accelerants, such as gasoline or kerosene, have been used and will prove whether a fire was the work of an arsonist or an accident. The area where the smell of accelerant is most highly concentrated is usually a safe bet for the origin of the fire in question, which means that sniffer dogs can be used to ascertain this information as well!

> TV shows depicting cyber crime often show the criminal in question deleting any incriminating evidence of his illegal cyber activities. Deleting data is often shown to be an all-purpose, foolproof way of ensuring that police will not be able to find any evidence of cyber crimes, allowing the perpetrator to run scot-free! As you might have guessed based on the nature of this list and all of its entries, the reality of the situation is far from the truth of the matter, as is experienced while practically applying forensic methodology to the scene of the crime. The fact of the matter is that there is an entire branch of forensic science that deals with computers, and forensic analysts working in this field are able to recover deleted files in no time. This is due to the fact that when you delete files from your computer, the data they possess is not removed from your hard drive. Rather, it is hidden and set aside to be overwritten when the disk space it is using up is required for some other form of data. Forensic analysts specializing in computers can use this to

their advantage and extract the "deleted" data from the area on the hard drive where it has been hidden, allowing authorities to secure evidence that has resulted in the incarceration of many cyber criminals.

➢ Judging by how often it is portrayed in popular culture as the only foolproof way of apprehending criminals, its not surprising that many people feel like forensic science is responsible for the most convictions out of any type of such tool used in the criminal justice system. However, it may surprise you to learn that this is not the case! Despite its solid reputation, forensic science and analysis is only the second most effective method of identifying and apprehending perpetrators of crimes. The most effective and reliable method of apprehending criminals is, in fact, eyewitness testimony. This is due to the fact that it is easier to believe that someone saw a crime being committed with their very own eyes than to believe the scientific opinion of a group of people who analyzed trace elements found at the crime scene and matched them to a suspect. However, it should be noted that eyewitness testimony is often entirely unreliable due to the fact that people are prone to forget things and alter memories in their own heads unwittingly to fit the narrative that the police are trying to tell. Poor lighting and quick movements also often result in witnesses being unsure of what they actually saw. Hence, eyewitness testimony is often bolstered with forensic analysis, where forensic evidence is used to corroborate what the eyewitnesses claim to have seen.

➢ As we have discussed, smell is often an extremely important aspect of forensic analysis. Based on this information, one can logically ascertain that other senses can come into play while attempting to forensically analyze a crime scene or the corpse of a murder victim. This is true. One sense apart from smell that can be used to ascertain the time of death for a corpse is sight. This is due to the fact that when a person dies, the blood in their body begins to descend and can easily be visually detected. This means that blood, no longer being circulated through the body by the heart, will begin to accumulate in the part of the body that is closest to the ground. This process is referred to as livor mortis and results in discoloration of the part of the body of the victim that is closest to the ground, as well as swelling of the flesh in that part of the body. Authorities can ascertain the victim's time of death by examining the amount of livor mortis that has occurred and calculating the amount of time that has passed based on the rate of blood flow. Hence, using one's eyes at the crime scene can help discover a very important detail about the victim of the crime in question, allowing authorities to apprehend the perpetrator of the crime a lot more quickly!

➤ Based on the fact that forensic science and analysis gained serious popularity only very recently in the twentieth century, many people assume that fingerprinting, one of the most important parts of forensic analysis, is also a recent invention. This is another common assumption that people make regarding an aspect of forensic science that is completely untrue! Although it is true that fingerprinting began to be used by police in matters of criminal law in the twentieth century, the unique grooves on the skin of the tips of one's fingers was used to identify people long ago in Chinese society, when education was considered a right of the elite and the elite alone, resulting in a highly educated royalty. However, this meant that the vast majority of the members of the lower classes did not know how to read or write, which meant that they were unable to write their own names. This caused problems when members of the lower classes were required to sign legal documents. Hence, the Chinese legal system required members of the lower classes to "sign" legal documents using their thumbprints instead, as they were well aware of the fact that the unique design left by the skin on one's fingers could help identify the person that had left the impression.

➢ Most people seem to think that their activities on the internet are a secret. This often allows people to be extremely rude to others on online forums, with certain people even threatening violence or sexual abuse because they feel safe behind their mask of assumed anonymity. However, despite the fact that you may feel as though your activities on the internet are known to no one but you, tracking people's online activities is not just possible, it is in fact one of the easiest ways to track and conduct surveillance on a person. Remember that the internet is basically a vast, interconnected public forum. This means that absolutely anybody can access it, even the authorities. There have been many cases where the government has commissioned specially trained forensic scientists to track the online activities of certain individuals. This occurs most often when the individual being monitored has been suspected of some kind of illegal activity, regardless of whether this illegal activity has been performed on the internet or in the physical world. Criminals that have been recently released from prison are also closely monitored online to ensure that they are not intending to perform any illegal activity again. The reason that this is so effective is that so much of our lives is now based on what we do online. From purchasing items to socializing, we do next to everything online, which means that if someone was planning to commit a crime, evidence of it can probably be found somewhere in their internet history.

➢ Another often believed assumption is that conducting forensic analysis is an extremely easy task. This is due to the fact that the TV programs that depict forensic analysis are usually no more than forty-five minutes long. Often the longest fictional portrayals of forensic analysis are films that are usually no more than two hours long. Neither of these run times is long enough to truly depict what a long and gruelling process forensic analysis can sometimes be, as they require the plot to be resolved in a timely manner; otherwise, the narrative would bore the viewer. The amount of time it takes to perform a forensic test usually depends on how technical the test in question is. For example, fingerprint analysis can be completed in a few minutes, thanks to the advanced computers that are now involved in the process. However, DNA analysis can take several days or even weeks. This is due to the fact that the analysis being performed is extremely precise in nature, which means that the tests must be conducted slowly and carefully, otherwise the results could be botched. At times, extra precautions must be taken to ensure that the result that is obtained is accurate to the fullest degree, something that further extends the time that is required to perform this type of analysis successfully. Hence, forensic analysis takes a lot longer than is shown on TV.

➢ Although forensic science is a science in the traditional sense, in that it is based on careful objective analysis of entities that must be preserved to acquire accurate results, learning how to become a forensic scientist involves a lot more than poring over complicated textbooks for hours on end. Instead, it involves practical application of skills learned on the job, which means that in order to learn how to become a forensic scientist, you must do what forensic scientists do and learn from your mistakes! Although textbooks can provide you with a basic understanding regarding what exactly forensic scientists do, to become a good forensic analyst you must apply the skills that you have been learning. This means that you will have to become involved in actual criminal investigations, something that can usually be accomplished by acquiring an internship with a police department or an independent forensics lab or becoming the apprentice of a fully qualified forensic scientist. However, not all aspiring forensic scientists are able to gain internships or apprenticeships in this way, as getting such an opportunity mostly requires luck and skill. Those who are not lucky enough to get such opportunities often have to resort to honing their skills by studying actual dead bodies, or cadavers. Doing so may seem off-putting for some, but for someone who wants to be a forensic scientist, doing so is only a stepping stone to something greater, a dream come true.

➤ Another common misconception that has become common as a result of depictions of forensic analysis on TV is that all evidence obtained at a crime scene is absolutely pristine and can be undoubtedly used to tie a suspect to the scene of the crime and later be used in court to convict the perpetrator of the crime that has been committed. However, the reality of the situation is far from the polished and pretty image that is depicted on TV. The fact of the matter is, as much as authorities would like to come to a crime scene that has been utterly uncontaminated, there are too many uncontrollable variables for this to be possible. The weather, passers-by, and wild animals—all of these things end up contaminating the crime scene and there is absolutely nothing that can be done about it. Evidence collected at crime scenes will undoubtedly be corrupted or contaminated in one way or another, which means that authorities have to make do with what they get, something that rarely ends up being useful as the case progresses. In a twist that is tragically ironic, violent crimes, arguably crimes that require the most attention, often contain the least amounts of usable evidence. This is due to the nature of the crime that has created the crime scene. Violence often results in things surrounding the altercation breaking apart, blood of the victim damaging trace evidence, or explosions resulting in destroyed crime scenes. All in all, evidence is much harder to come by than is shown on TV.

> Forensic science is not just used to solve criminal cases here in the present day. Time travel is possible in a way using forensic science, because it is often used to solve cold cases. Cold cases are essentially those cases that occurred in the past and have essentially "gone cold" without a successful conviction. This was often due to the fact that technology was simply not advanced enough in the time period where the crime occurred to be able to successfully tie the perpetrator to the scene of the crime. An example is the Ripper case, where if DNA analysis had existed, a conviction would almost certainly have been made. In particular, DNA analysis is often used to shed light on cold cases, as well-preserved DNA evidence can now be analyzed to learn more about the criminal. Hence, forensic science and analysis can be used to solve cold cases, or, in situations where the evidence is insufficient or was improper-

ly stored, at the very least new information can be learned about these cases, which might aid them getting solved later on. Such cold case investigations conducted in the present day can also be conducted on investigations that were closed but the conviction was widely suspected to be incorrect. In this way, people that were convicted of crimes that they had not committed can be, and are, exonerated of their charges.

Famous Cold Cases Solved Using Forensic Science

Throughout the years as it grew as discipline, forensic science has been known to help greatly in the solving of cold cases. Cold cases are essentially cases that are shelved because there is insufficient evidence to either narrow down a perpetrator or if police suspect who committed the crime, obtain a conviction. Forensic analysis allows closer examination of evidence that was impossible at the time of the crime, but is now possible due to the advancement of technology. The following cases were solved using methods of forensic analysis.

Krystal Beslanowitch

The story of Krystal Beslanowitch[xlvi] is a landmark in the realm of forensic science because it is one of the most widely publicized cold cases solved using forensic methodology.

Krystal was seventeen years old in 1995 when her corpse, bloody and entirely nude, was found by a jogger on the bank of the Provo River in the state of Utah. Although she was initially classified as a Jane Doe, information was quickly discovered about her,

Krystal Beslanowitch

and she was traced to her parents who were living in Spokane, Washington at the time.

Krystal's body, being discovered so far away from her hometown, was a result of the lifestyle that she was leading. According to her mother, Krystal had strayed off the straight and narrow path early on in her life. At the age of fifteen, she had become addicted to various drugs and began working as a prostitute to fund her drug habit. This eventually led to her running off with her boyfriend, and they made their way to Salt Lake City. However, the circumstances that led to her murder were still unclear.

Krystal Beslanowitch went missing a few months after she arrived in Salt Lake City. She left to buy some groceries at a local convenience store and virtually disappeared. After several hours lapsed, her boyfriend eventually phoned the authorities and described her to them. When Krystal was eventually found, her boyfriend's call to the authorities, and his description of her, was instrumental in helping the authorities identify who she was. Unfortunately, the investigators still did not have much to go on based on the crime scene.

The place she was found was a veritable nightmare for any seasoned investigator who hoped to arrive at a crime scene that was in pristine condition and devoid of any degradation or corruption. This was not a pristine crime scene. The water had washed much of the evidence away, covering it up with mud and rocks, and, of course, the inevitable passersby had unwittingly done their share of contamination. What little evidence that could be gleaned from the crime scene was not nearly enough to give the investigators anything beyond a few weak leads which, after extensive pursuit, were eventually dropped and the case went cold as a result.

The only real lead Detective Todd Bonner had to go on was his own psychological analysis of the UNSUB (unknown subject). The murderer had killed Krystal by crushing her skull with a rock, an exceedingly brutal way to kill somebody. This led Bonner to infer that the killer had problems with anger and had likely killed before. Because Krystal's skull had been crushed completely, without hesitation and with passion, rather than partially crushed, he believed the killer had experience with murder.

However, this was simply not enough to go on, and with so little evidence to give Bonner any leads, the case was eventually laid to rest and added to the long list of murders that went unsolved.

The solving of this case can be attributed to two distinct entities: the first of these two is a significant advancement in DNA analysis[xlvii] in the first decade of the twenty-first century, and the second is Bonner's compassion, dedication and empathy.

One piece of evidence that was taken from the body of the victim was DNA from underneath her fingernails. This, the authorities concluded, was the skin of the assailant, which Krystal had scratched off as she had attempted to defend herself from her attacker. DNA was also found on the bloody rock that had been left near the victim's corpse, this DNA being touch DNA, essentially organic matter that the assailant left on the murder weapon as he was committing the deed. However, nothing could be done with this evidence, as DNA analysis was simply not advanced enough in 1995 to allow investigators to get any workable leads at the time the case was being pursued. This led to the case running cold after two years. This is where the importance of advancements made in the field of DNA analysis comes in.

Eventually, DNA fingerprinting got to the point where it became the single most successful method of forensic analysis in the world, making DNA one of the most important pieces of evidence that could be found at a crime scene. Hence, a breakthrough was made when the DNA found on the murder weapon was put through the database seventeen years later, when the technology was advanced enough, and Bonner was finally able to find a match.

However, it is important to note that a breakthrough would simply not have been possible had the second important entity not existed, this being Bonner's empathy and compassion. He felt for Krystal, and believed she was simply misguided and doing whatever she could to survive. The case had haunted him in the years that followed. He eventually managed to move on, going on to become the sheriff of his county, but his inability to solve the murder of a girl he felt was innocent and undeserving of such an end led in no small way to the eventual apprehending of her murderer.

When Bonner realized that DNA evidence

had advanced to such a point where the evidence found so many years earlier could determine Krystal's murderer, he hopped on the chance and ran the DNA found on the rock through the DNA database. To his great surprise, it came up with a perfect match. Bonner's deduction that the killer had murdered before was right. Krystal's killer's DNA matched a convicted killer in the DNA database.

This gave Bonner enough cause to open the case but not enough to convict the man whose DNA had matched, a man by the name of Joseph Simpson, who had been convicted of murder in the early 1980s, but was released prior to the year in which Krystal's murder was committed. The DNA collected after Simpson's murder conviction in the 1980s was not enough because, according to prosecutors, the sample it was matched to was far too old to be taken seriously by any judge or jury. Additionally, the suspect was living in Florida at the time his DNA was matched with the DNA found on the murder weapon used to kill Krystal, and according to Florida state law, Bonner would not have nearly enough time to arrest Simpson, obtain a DNA sample, and match it to the DNA found on the murder weapon.

Bonner resorted to good old-fashioned sleuthing, and he deserves full credit for the way the DNA was obtained. Enlisting help from Florida detectives, Bonner tailed Simpson tirelessly. He discovered what Simpson's job was and that he lived with his mother, but the true breakthrough came one day when Simpson went to a local convenience store. He purchased a pack of cigarettes, one of which he smoked and disposed of before walking away. This cigarette ended up being the key to what happened next.

It didn't take Bonner long to pick that cigarette butt up after Simpson had left. Since Simpson had put his mouth on the cigarette filter, saliva was present, and in this saliva was Simpson's DNA. This ended up providing enough DNA evidence to get a definitive match with the DNA that had been taken from the murder weapon all those years ago when Krystal had been found on that riverbank. Hence, Bonner now had enough evidence to make an arrest.

Joseph Simpson did not resist arrest and was fairly talkative during his interrogation, but he refused to confess to the murder or speak of his involvement in any murders or crimes.

Nevertheless, Simpson was eventually convicted in Krystal Beslanowitch's murder and the case was laid to rest. Bonner was able to finally call the girl's parents and tell them that the man who had murdered their daughter in such a brutal manner had finally been identified, arrested, and convicted. Both of Beslanowitch's parents and Bonner himself were able to move on with their lives, thanks to advancements in forensic analysis that allowed the intrepid criminal investigator to finally close a case that had begun to wear on him.

Michael Simpson

Lucille Johnson

The murder of Lucille Johnson was also committed in Utah, this time firmly within the city limits of Salt Lake City. The type of victim, however, is wildly different from Krystal Beslanowitch. Whereas Beslanowitch was a teenager, a drug addict, and a prostitute, and her murder had a distinct sexual motive, Lucille Johnson was, perhaps, the polar opposite in all regards. She was, first and foremost, not a teenager. She was seventy-two years old. The victim's personality was also highly different in this case, as Johnson was a church going woman and a well-respected member of the community.[xlviii]

The murder in this case was also markedly more brutal, with violence, not sexuality, taking center stage this time around. Although Beslanowitch was murdered in a matter that was cruel, her head being smashed by a rock, it pales when compared to the way in which Johnson was killed. Due to the blunt force trauma applied by her assailant, her body was virtually unrecognizable when she was found.

Lucille Johnson

Johnson was killed in the year 1991. Her daughter, who had become concerned by the fact that her mother had not been answering her phone and decided to pay her a visit, found her body in her bedroom. What she found was devastating. Her mother was lying on the bed with a pillow covering her face, and blood soaked through her bed sheets and the clothes she was wearing. Her body was mangled as if every bone had been broken.

Johnson's daughter called the police and

the story made it to the local news, due to the fact that the victim of this crime was such a well-respected member of society. Unfortunately, Lucille's son heard about his mother's death on the radio before his sister had time to inform him about what had happened to their mother.

As in the case of Beslanowitch, authorities were unable to find enough evidence at the scene of the crime and therefore didn't have much to go on with respect to determining who could have committed this crime. Through forensic analysis via an autopsy, investigators were able to determine that the cause of death had been a combination of blunt force trauma and strangulation but, apart from that, were not able to learn enough to generate any workable leads.

However, it can be argued that the evidence they did find was, in fact, enough to find out who had committed this atrocious act, if only science had been advanced enough back when the murder was committed in 1991 to properly analyze it. The investigators that had been assigned this case can also be forgiven for not realizing that the evidence in their possession could be useful due to the fact that, at first glance, it could not be considered particularly useful in the context of criminal investigative procedure.

This piece of evidence was a Lego that was found in the living room of Johnson's home. Obviously, the presence of a Lego in the living room was a minor detail as far as the case was concerned. Eventually, due to a lack of scientific advancement to facilitate the successful analysis of the evidence that the authorities were able to find, the case went cold and remained so for over two decades. However, the brutal nature of this case, the bludgeoning and strangulation of an innocent elderly woman by a perpetrator that could hardly be called human, meant that the investigators involved in the case were never able to move on completely, as the details of the case continued to haunt them throughout the years.

Fast-forward over two decades and, suddenly, the evidence that had seemed unimportant and was only stored for posterity's sake suddenly became the key element of the investigation. The reopening of the case was the result of something that, it is fair to say, the investigators lucked into: testimony volunteered by the wife of the then unidentified perpetrator, a man by the name of John Sansing. The very fact that the perpetrator's wife was now testifying at her husband's murder trial was because murder was, for him, a habit rather than a one-time occurrence.

As a result of the perpetrator's murderous tendencies, he found himself eventually getting apprehended for a completely different murder that had been committed seven years after he had killed Johnson. While in custody for this murder, his wife was interrogated and confessed that she knew her husband had murdered an elderly woman in Salt Lake City in 1991.

This confession led authorities to reopen Lucille Johnson's case, but it was one particular detail that the perpetrator's wife divulged later that led to the confirmation that her husband was the murderer. His wife informed authorities that he had taken their child along with him the day he had murdered Johnson.

It did not take long for authorities to put two and two together. Sansing's son would have been five years old in 1991 when Lucille Johnson had been murdered. This meant that he had probably been playing with the Lego piece in the living room, or had been the one who had brought the Lego along in the first place. Authorities deduced that the child had been in the living room while his father committed murder in the bedroom and had thus been playing with the Lego at the time. Since young children have a tendency to place any object they can into their mouths, authorities deduced that the child's saliva could have made contact with the Lego, and thus DNA would be present on it, which they could match to Sansing.

This is where the infinitely useful and veritably revolutionary forensic technique of DNA profiling came into play. Forensic scientists were able to extract DNA from the piece of Lego that had been found at the crime scene. Although the DNA did belong to Sansing's son rather than Sansing himself, it is important to note, as has been mentioned before, that DNA of family members can often be matched to the DNA of suspects. In some cases this causes confusion, as getting matches on somebody's DNA often implicates the person the sample originated from in the crime. However, in this case the DNA sample was from a five-year-old, allowing authorities to bypass bureaucracy and solve the case.

A sample from Sansing was obtained and compared to the DNA obtained from the Lego block. The result was a match, which proved that Sansing had been at the scene of the crime the day the murder had been committed. This was enough evidence to allow a judge to convict the man of murder in the first degree.

The verdict did not really affect the perpetrator of this heinous crime, since Sansing was already on death row for a murder he had committed in 1998, an unrelated murder that nevertheless led to closure in the case of Lucille Johnson. However, despite the fact that Sansing's sentence could not be made any more severe now that it had been proved he was responsible for the death of Lucille Johnson as well, it at least allowed the victim's children to gain closure, as well as the investigators involved in the case who had been haunted by the gruesome crime for decades.

There are still a couple of mysteries surrounding the case. Even though it was proven conclusively that Sansing was, in fact, the perpetrator of the murder, certain details regarding the overall situation remained hazy even after the conviction. For example, how did Sansing enter Lucille Johnson's home? How did he make it all the way into the bedroom? And what was his son doing there? And why would Sansing want to murder a woman to begin with?

It has been speculated that these questions are interlinked. The presence of Sansing's son may have been a ploy to get the victim to trust him. The presence of a child does present a wholesome image, so Sansing might have used his son in a ruse to get the victim to let him into her home, perhaps claiming that the child was hurt or needed help in some way, or that he required help unrelated to the child but the presence of said child made his plight seem more genuine than it would have seemed otherwise. Once inside, Sansing probably attacked his victim, incapacitating her and taking her to the bedroom where he beat and killed her.

The answer to why Sansing would do this remains a mystery. The man was a sociopath, and Lucille Johnson was probably a random victim. However, her murderer was convicted of his crime and did not go free, all thanks to the forensic methodology used to connect him to the murder. Without DNA profiling, the victim's children would never have found out who killed their mother and would thus have been unable to receive the closure they deserved.

Sara Lynn Wineski

Cold case murders are often considered to be few and far between nowadays. They are believed to be anomalies in a world where forensic science can tie virtually any murderer to virtually any crime. This, however, is far from the truth, as this case will prove.

There are many murder cases that have gone cold. Cold cases are, in fact, extremely common, not for the more well-established and well-off members of society, but for a segment of society far more disenfranchised: the homeless. Indeed, it is the homeless and the poor that are most often the victims of violence and whose murderers often go unpunished. This can be blamed on two things.

First, no one really seems to care about the homeless. The general narrative in society is that they had their chance and they blew it, thereby deserving all of the suffering they are currently enduring, including the perpetual threat of dying a violent death. This leads to a general attitude of disinterest among law enforcement officials who are assigned cases in which a homeless person has been murdered. This has become endemic to the point where getting assigned a homeless murder is a punishment of sorts in police departments. This negative perception is also a result of the low closing rate of homeless murder cases.

Homeless murders are also quite difficult to solve. There are often few to no witnesses, and the witnesses that police officers do find are often incoherent or cannot be presented as reliable witnesses in court. As a result, the murders of homeless people often go cold with no one seeming to care about them like they do about the cold cases of the two aforementioned victims.

However, this changed in the case of a homeless woman named Sara Lynn Wineski,[xlix] who was found strangled and raped under a table in an uninhabited building in the city of St. Petersburg, Florida. Law enforcement officials were informed of her murder after several residents of the area reported screaming in the middle of the night. This case is very different from the two that have been previously covered. This is due to the fact that a suspect was identified only two years after the crime was committed, and the eventual apprehension of said suspect was the result of years of slowly piecing together the evidence via increasingly advanced forensic techniques, rather than a single eureka moment that sent all of the dominos tumbling.

Sara Lynn Wineski

Eyewitness testimony led law enforcement officials to identify Raymond Samuels as a suspect. Samuels had been in the same city as Wineski for about two months during the time when the murder was committed. The night when Wineski was murdered, residents of the area heard screaming and were able to spot Samuels running from the scene of the crime. The next day when authorities canvassed the area and asked questions, several people stated that they saw a man fleeing from the area.

Getting descriptions of the man from the witnesses, police were able to canvass popular spots in which homeless people tended to congregate. After viewing a rough sketch drawn from the descriptions of the perpetrator, several homeless people identified the man to be a transient by the name of Raymond Samuels who had arrived in St Petersburg around a month and a half ago, but had left recently.

A relative lull in the case followed. For around a year and a half, law enforcement officials tried without much success to locate Samuels, but to no avail. Eventually, they discovered that he had been apprehended for an unrelated crime, an attempted rape and murder, and was serving twenty-nine years in a Florida State Penitentiary.

Raymond Samuels was identified as a suspect in Wineski's murder through DNA that had been left at the crime scene. Rape is a terrible crime, and its victims often suffer lasting psychological damage, but they are often easy crimes to solve due to the fact that so much DNA can be collected from the scene of the crime.

Semen samples collected during a post-mortem examination of Wineski gave authorities a DNA sample that they could compare to their suspect's DNA. After obtaining a sample from Samuels, an analysis was made followed by a comparison. The result was a match. However, it was not enough to prove that Samuels had murdered Wineski, only that the two of them had sex. Since Samuels claimed that they had done so and it was consensual, there was no way for law enforcement officials to prove him wrong.

What followed was a slow and steady build up of evidence against Samuels. Credit must be given to the authorities in this regard, for they were fully aware of the fact that, since this was a homeless murder, they would have to build an airtight case to be able to convict Samuels of the horrible crime he had committed.

Thus, fingerprints was carefully extracted from the crime scene, corrupted though they were, further DNA was extracted from the victim's body and analyzed, as was DNA from Samuels. A veritable forensic master class was displayed as law enforcement officials and forensic scientists used every method at their disposal to apprehend this criminal.

Eventually, DNA samples were discovered not just in the form of semen on Wineski's body but on the scene of the crime as well. This was enough to prove that Samuels was present at the scene of the crime, something that proved to be a huge leap forward in building the case against him. However, despite the fact that law enforcement officials had proven that Samuels had been present at the scene of the crime, prosecutors informed them that it was still not enough to convict Samuels of the murder of Sara Lynn Wineski, due to the fact that it was circumstantial. Samuels could claim that he and the victim had had sex at that location and she was murdered after he left, and there would be no evidence to prove he was lying.

Hence, law enforcement officials had to

begin their forensic analysis once again. The murder weapon that had been used by the perpetrator had been a belt, and law enforcement officials deduced that DNA was probably present on this as well, due to the messy nature of the crime. They performed DNA analysis on the belt, hoping this would be their one piece of breakthrough evidence. After several weeks of analysis, forensic scientists were able to extract two DNA samples from the murder weapon. One of these samples belonged to Wineski and the other belonged to Samuels.

Just to be sure that their evidence stood up in court, law enforcement officials obtained a fresh sample of DNA from Samuels. This DNA turned out to match the second DNA sample obtained from the murder weapon. Finally possessing enough evidence, the police in charge of this case took their evidence to the state prosecutors. The case was judged to be airtight.

Upon examining all of the evidence obtained through forensic analysis, the judge presiding over the court deemed Samuels to be guilty of the murder of Sara Lynn Wineski.

Her case brought much attention to the plight of homeless women, particularly in St. Petersburg. As a result of the advancement of DNA profiling techniques as well as other methods of forensic analysis, a murderer and rapist was put behind bars. Had it not been for forensic science, Samuels would never have been convicted of the rape and murder of Sara Lynn Wineski.

It should be noted here that forensic analysis is not just the realm of shots in the dark and eureka moments. A steady build up of evidence and the slow creation of an airtight case can be made possible through the use of forensic analysis. This case shows just how important forensic analysis has been in law enforcement, and how important it is in the solving of cold cases in particular.

Yolanda Sapp, Nicki Lowe and Kathleen Brisbois

The case of Yolanda Sapp, Nicki Lowe and Kathleen Brisbois[i] can once again be used to objectively analyze how difficult it is to solve cases involving prostitutes. The three women were each killed at various times during the year of 1990. A .22-caliber handgun was used to kill all three of them. After being shot, each of the women was dragged and dumped in various areas around the Spokane River.

Yolanda Sapp, Nicki Lowe, and Kathleen Brisbois

Yolanda Sapp had been found on February 22, 1990, at East Upriver Drive. The twenty-six-year-old had been nude and blindfolded at the time of her death. Forensic analysts conducting a postmortem exam ascertained that she had been shot three times, which had been the cause of her death.

Nicki Lowe, the second victim to be discovered, was thirty-four years old and was found in South Riverton on March 25, 1990. She had also been shot, but she was not found nude, nor had she been blindfolded. The only things missing from her person were one of the tennis shoes that she had been wearing and her red billfold. Additionally, she had only been shot once, whereas Sapp had been shot several times. Although the discovery of another murdered woman only a month after one had been discovered in a nearby area should have seemed suspicious, the fact that Lowe was clothed and Sapp had been nude threw law enforcement officials off the scent.

Thirty-eight-year-old Kathleen Brisbois was the oldest of the three prostitutes that were killed. She was discovered along the Spokane River itself. The circumstances of her death were similar to that of Sapp, as she was found nude with three gunshot wounds, which had been the cause of her death. Additionally, various articles of her clothing were found in the surrounding area, indicating that she had been brought to the location, undressed along the way, and shot dead at the very spot she was eventually found.

Initially, each of the women was discovered without any form of identification and thus given the status of Jane Does. However, each time authorities performed postmortem analysis on the victims, they were able to either extract DNA or obtain fingerprints and run it through their respective databases to ascertain these women's identities.

Law enforcement officials were initially unaware that these murders were related. It was only when the identities of the victims revealed that they all worked as prostitutes, that a connection was made. This was due to the fact that it is essential to establish a similar background shared by victims before it can be proven that they were killed by a serial murderer, as choosing victims that are similar in some way is a universal aspect of every serial killer's modus operandi.

Although it was now clear that each of these women had been murdered under similar circumstances and they were probably victims of a serial murderer, forensic technology was not advanced enough to analyze the trace evidence that had been discovered at the crime scene. This was due to the fact that, at the time, DNA analysis in general was a very new science, and thus forensic scientists were still unaware of its true potential.

DNA was discovered to be a unique identifier for an individual in the mid-1980s, and hence was only about five years old when these murders occurred. Even though the law enforcement officials that had been assigned the case had been able to obtain evidence that could pinpoint the very person that had committed the crimes, there were two major problems at play here. First and foremost, they had no suspect from which they could obtain a sample of DNA to compare to the evidence they had obtained from the scene of each crime. Additionally, and more significantly, since there was no unified database of each individual's unique DNA yet, it was not possible for law enforcement officials to run the sample obtained from the crime scene through said database to come up with a match, a thing that is taken for granted these days now that it has become so (relatively) easy. As a result of the inferiority of forensic technology at the time, the case went cold.

As is the case with most cold cases later cracked by forensic technology, advances and innovations in the field of DNA analysis eventually allowed the case to be reopened in the year 2005. Thanks to the fact that the DNA evidence obtained during the initial investigation had been stored safely by the forensic scientists in the original case and could still be used, the detectives assigned to the case, two men by the names of Mark Burbridge and Jim Dresbeck, had something to go on.

Burbridge and Dresbeck provided the DNA evidence to a nearby crime lab and asked them to run it through their DNA database. After four years, the crime lab was able to ascertain certain details about the individual that had committed the murder, including the fact that he was a male along with certain general characteristics that the individual would possess. A suspect profile was developed and submitted to the Combined DNA Index System, or CODIS, which is a compilation of all DNA profiles of convicted offenders in local, federal, and state databases. CODIS is essentially the Wikipedia of DNA in a way, as it possesses all DNA profiles of convicted criminals in any database in the USA.

Through CODIS, the forensic analysts at this crime lab were able to get a match on the DNA found on some of the evidence from a man by the name of Douglas Perry. This match took three whole years after a full profile had been developed. Including the time it took to create the DNA profile itself, the whole process took a whopping seven years to complete. This shows just how time consuming DNA analysis can be when law enforcement officials don't have a suspect to obtain a sample from, or when the DNA obtained from a crime scene must be used to find a suspect in the first place.

Perry, as it turned out, was already in custody at the SeaTac Detention Facility after being arrested for possessing unlawful firearms and ammunition. When Dresdeck and Burbridge went to interrogate Perry, they happened upon two pieces of information, both of which were vital but one in particular that was shocking to say the least.

Douglas Perry

The first piece of information that they obtained when they made it to the detention center was in regards to his criminal history. Perry had been involved in a number of altercations between the years 1974 and 1988. This led to a number of assault and weapons charges against him, which made it illegal for him to have any kind of firearm or ammunition in his possession. He was also arrested for soliciting the services of a prostitute in the year 1989, only six months before Yolanda Sapp was found dead. All of this information told Dresdeck and Burbridge that Perry was a violent man who had begun to develop a taste for prostitutes right before the first victim was found, both of which made him a prime suspect in their case.

The second piece of information had little to do with the case but everything to do with Perry and his mental state. This information that they learned after meeting the man was that he was not, in fact, a man at all anymore, but a woman. Douglas Perry had undergone a sex change surgery in Bangkok, Thailand in the year 2000, now identified as Donna Perry and was, for all intents and purposes, a woman.

Perry attempted to use the fact that he was now a woman to defend himself. He claimed that he had undergone the sex change operation as an attempt to curb his violent tendencies, as women have far fewer violent tendencies than men do. Despite the fact that Perry's claims were specious at best, his words worked in his favour and he was granted a small amount of clemency. Perry's defense made the judge ask for more evidence that Perry had committed these crimes, as the DNA evidence connecting Perry to the murders only proved that he had procured the services of these prostitutes, not that he had killed them.

This request for more evidence ended up working in the prosecution's favour. Perry was notorious for his proclivity for weapons, and because of this, he had been arrested several times on federal firearms charges. In the year 1988, Perry had been arrested for possessing a pipe bomb, and he was arrested once again in 1994 for the unlawful possession of firearms and ammunition.

After each arrest, Perry's home was searched. After the 1988 arrest, forty-nine fire-arms with a thousand rounds of ammunition each were discovered in his home. The 1994 search, on the other hand, was less fruitful. However, in both cases a .22-caliber gun was found in his home, the same kind of gun that had killed each of the three prostitutes in 1990.

The newest firearm charge that Perry had been arrested for gave Federal law enforce-ment officials the right to search his place of residence once more. The Bureau of Alcohol, Tobacco, Firearms and Explosives, also known as the ATF, was the agency responsi-ble for Perry's previous arrests and all previ-ous searches of his home. The same was true this time around.

When the ATF searched Perry's home they found a lot of weapons and ammunition, enough to put Perry away on his third strike, but nothing that indicated that Perry was responsible for the Sapp, Lowe and Brisbois murders. However, ATF Agent Todd Smith noticed that the closet door in Perry's bedroom had been painted shut. Once the door was open and firearms were not found, the ATF agents began to look elsewhere. Since the search was focused on finding arms and ammunition, the content of the closets not pertaining to the search criteria was largely ignored.

Agent Smith noticed something that would eventually become very important to Perry's eventual conviction. This important detail was a box that he found to be full of women's underwear. The underwear was far too small to belong to Perry, but what truly caught Smith's eye was how they had been positioned. They did not look like articles of clothing, rather they looked like trophies. They looked like the kind of trophies a serial killer would keep when they wanted to relive their crime.

A month later, when the items found in Perry's place of residence were inventoried, the final break occurred that allowed Dresdeck and Burbridge to seal the case. In a dumpster near Perry's place of residence, Nickie Lowe's tennis shoe and billfold were found by a local resident, as well as a tube of jelly. From this tube, forensic scientists were able to obtain a fingerprint that matched Perry's.

This was the final nail in the coffin. In the face of so much overwhelming evidence, the jury unanimously convicted Perry guilty of the murders. The importance of fingerprinting and DNA analysis cannot be expressed. Without DNA analysis, Perry would never have been found, and after he had been found, convicting him would have been nearly impossible had it not been for fingerprint analysis. This case proves once again how important forensic analysis is to the solving of reopened cold cases.

Patricia Beard

The Denver Cold Case Team[li] is a division of sorts of the Denver Police Department that works in concert with the District Attorney's office operating in that particular area. This team is one of the finest collections of forensic scientists in the world, and its members pride themselves on their ability to crack cold cases through forensic methodology. Funded by federal grants, the team is free to pursue cold cases based on merit, which allows them to solve the cases that they feel are most deserving of being solved.

This is a breath of fresh air in a world where money is everything. Entire companies have sprung up that hire forensic scientists and offer their services in exchange for exorbitant fees. This continues the inherent social narrative that rich people are more important because it is only rich people that are able to afford to pay these fees. As a result, cold cases in which the relatives of wealthy people, members of the upper class essentially, are involved are often solved fairly quickly after they go cold. Cold cases involving poor people on the other hand, cases usually involving far more heinous crimes, tend to go unsolved for decades at a time.

This is very sad when you take into account the fact that poor people are usually murdered, raped, and assaulted in ways far more violent than rich people are, due to the fact that there is a generally vitriolic societal narrative at work against them. Because the Denver Cold Case Team is funded by the federal government, they are therefore free to pursue these more violent cases simply because the victims and their relatives deserve justice and the closure and peace of mind that comes with it.

One of the most important cases that this team has solved happens to be their 100th case relating to rape or murder. Apart from the fact that this was a significant landmark in the history of the cold case team—getting a hundred of anything is often celebrated as a significant sign of success—it is its nature that makes this particular case so important.

The victim in question this time was Patricia Beard[lii] and it is easy to see why her brutal rape and murder garnered so much sympathy from the media and law enforcement officials. You see, thirty-two-year-old Patricia Beard was a mentally disabled African American woman. People just don't want to hear about African Americans being killed, or so the media thinks, and so white people getting murdered tend to get far more coverage. The case of Patricia Beard, however, was different because she was a person living with mental disability.

Beard lived alone in an apartment that was part of a group home for mentally disabled people, and her family often called to check up on her. Obviously since she was mentally disabled, they became incredibly worried when they were unable to reach her. Hence, when he failed to contact Patricia for several days, a member of the family went up to the East Denver facility

Patricia Beard

where she lived on March 27, 1981. What he saw shocked him, to say the least.

Patricia was discovered face up on her bed. Her pink robe had been torn open, and her panties were around her ankles. A few feet away was a used tampon that looked like it had been tossed aside, and her slip had been pushed up over her genital area and was around her waist. She had clearly been raped. Upon closer examination, Patricia's relative also saw that she had been murdered.

The police were called and the facility was cordoned off. Upon examination of the crime scene, law enforcement officials were able to deduce that her killer had climbed up to her apartment using an exterior pipe and had entered through an open window. There had been a struggle, after which the killer had been able to incapacitate Patricia, rape her, and kill her.

Patricia's body was examined, and in the postmortem examination conducted by the forensic scientists attached to this case, the general damage that had been caused to her body was ascertained. This damage included a deep cut to her left breast, fractured bones throughout her body, probably stemming from the violent way in which she had been incapacitated, and severe hemorrhaging around her neck. The hemorrhaging told the forensic scientists examining the body that the cause of death had been strangulation.

Once the cause of death had been ascertained, trace evidence was compiled. This evidence included fingerprints, DNA, and fibres. However, as is the situation with virtually all cold cases, despite the fact that authorities had a large amount of DNA, they were unable to do anything with it simply because technology wasn't advanced enough. In this case, DNA analysis hadn't even been invented yet, let alone advanced enough, to discover who had murdered Patricia Beard.

The fingerprints that were obtained from the crime scene were put through the FBI fingerprint database but without any luck. It appeared as if the perpetrator of Beard's murder had never been convicted for a criminal offense—in other words, his fingerprints were not in the system.

Since the trace evidence found at the crime scene was useless and there were no witnesses to talk about what had happened, the case quickly went cold. A wrench was thrown into any future attempts to solve this case when the majority of the evidence from the case was disposed of in 1994, when the police department needed to make room for new evidence.

Thirty years passed and eventually Patricia Beard's murder was virtually forgotten about after being chalked up to just one of those murders that no one would be able to solve. The media furor had died down long ago when the case failed to generate any new leads. Members of the Beard family, after the killer of their relative escaped justice, were forced to console themselves with the thought that their beloved Patricia was now at peace. However, in the year 2011, a detective working for the Denver Cold Case Unit discovered a postmortem kit made by the forensic scientist that had been working on Patricia Beard's case. This postmortem kit contained so much evidence, the detective realized it could be used to reignite the case.

With the new evidence, the detective approached a forensic scientist and asked him to analyze the contents of the postmortem kit. In this kit there were two cotton swabs, one that possessed DNA obtained from the victim's vagina and another one that possessed DNA obtained from the victim's mouth. After extensive testing was conducted on each of these cotton swabs, it was found that a significant amount of DNA from each of the swabs was semen. This was an important development as it revealed to the detective that the killer had performed oral as well as vaginal sex with Patricia.

The detective decided to request that a DNA profile of the suspect be made using this DNA, similar to the technique Detectives Dresdeck and Burbridge used in the case of Sapp, Lowe and Brisbois. Fortunately, the same DNA profile build up that took forensic scientists 4 years to create in 2005 took only a single year in 2011.

Despite the efficiency to build a DNA profile this time round, the detective failed to find a suspect. This lack of a result occurred for the same reason that law enforcement officials failed to find a match for the fingerprints they had found at the crime scene: the perpetrator of Patricia Beard's rape and murder had never been convicted of a federal offense, which meant that his DNA simply wasn't in the system.

Since this is a detective from the fine institution of the Denver Cold Case Team we are talking about, the case was not allowed to go cold again. The DNA profile was checked against CODIS repeatedly until finally, on July 11, 2013, a match was found. It took the length of Patricia Beard's entire lifetime for a suspect to be named in her murder.

Hector Bencomo-Hinojos

The suspect was a man by the name of Hector Bencomo-Hinojos. The reason that a match was finally made was due to the fact that Bencomo-Hinojos had finally been arrested for a federal offense. This also made him easy to find, since he was now serving time at a federal penitentiary in Loretto, Pennsylvania. The killer's subsequent interrogation proved to be far less than fruitful, owing to the fact that he stubbornly refused to know anything about... well, anything.

When asked whether he knew the victim, Bencomo-Hinojos claimed that he had never seen her before in his life. When asked whether he had performed sexual acts, both oral and vaginal, with her, Bencomo-Hinojos proved to be either amazingly stubborn or amazingly ignorant. He flat-out denied that he'd ever had any form of sex with her and went on to deny ever having had sex with a woman of African American ethnicity. His denial of knowing anything about the incident stretched to the point where he even denied any knowledge regarding oral sex, claiming to know very little about the sexual technique.

The real shocker came when the Denver Cold Case Team detective asked him if he knew who had murdered Patricia Beard. Bencomo-Hinojos claimed that he did know what the word murder meant.

It was obvious that the detective was not going to get anywhere interrogating Bencomo-

Hinojos, so he decided to go and talk to the man's former wife. This interview proved to be significantly more fruitful. This was due to the fact that Bencomo-Hinojos's former wife was extremely unsatisfied with the way her husband had treated her during the time they had been married.

Bencomo-Hinojos's former wife claimed that her husband had often been violent with her, slapping and shoving her around. She provided detailed medical reports of times she had spent in the hospital after instances where her husband would get particularly violent with her. These medical reports also showed that Bencomo-Hinojos had been very violent sexually as well. All of this proved that Bencomo-Hinojos was the type of man who would rape and murder a disabled woman.

The final statement from Bencomo-Hinojos's wife that cast her former husband as the most probable killer of Patricia Beard was the fact that he had a tendency to steal. She stated that he often came home with items of value such as silverware or electronic items and would claim that he was keeping them for some friend or the other. She was reasonably sure that he committed burglaries. This proved that Bencomo-Hinojos had the skill set required to climb up to the first floor of a building and commit the crime he was now being suspected of.

With a fresh DNA sample obtained from Bencomo-Hinojos that matched the DNA on the cotton swabs, as well as his wife's testimony in court, the man was convicted of murder. Without DNA analysis and the significant advances it has made in recent years, the murder and rape of Patricia Beard would have never been solved. Credit must also be given to the Denver Cold Case Team, who is proving with each cold case they solve just how useful forensic science can be in all aspects of the criminal investigative system. This is proven by the fact that this team, using only forensic science, has solved more cold cases than any other law enforcement agency in the world.

Anna Palmer

It is often said that Salt Lake City is the home to more cold cases than any other city. Certainly it features more than any other city on this list. Perhaps it is the nature of this city's demographic that causes this statistical anomaly to develop. The same racial narrative exists in Salt Lake City that exists everywhere else. The poor and the rich have the same vitriolic attitudes towards each other, the same as anywhere else. Yet there is something unique about this city, a vibe similar to that of Derry, Maine, a fictional city invented by author Stephen King and home to the majority of his plots.

Salt Lake City seems similarly eventful. It is as though the melting pot of this city's unique cultural history, its specific cultural narrative distinct from that of the rest of America, has resulted in either a higher amount of cases running out of leads and going cold, or a higher amount of cold cases later reopened and solved thanks to advancing methods of forensic analysis. The cold cases don't even pertain to a single demographic. Krystal Beslanowitch was a young prostitute, Lucille Johnson was an elderly woman and a respectable member of society, and the third victim residing in Salt Lake City at the time of her death, whose cold case was later solved using forensic methodology, is as wildly different from the aforementioned victims as they are from her.

Anna Palmer

The name of this victim is Anna Palmer.[liii] Her mother found her dead on the front porch of her home on a warm summer evening in the year 1999 after returning home from work. At 5:00 p.m., ten-year-old Anna had called her mother and asked her if she could go to a friend's place. At 7:00 p.m., when her mother returned, she found her daughter lying on the front porch. She later described her daughter as looking waxy and yellow, with her face appearing as if her blood was no longer flowing within her. Upon touching her hand and finding it cold, the victim's mother called 911 immediately.

When the ambulance arrived, the paramedics attempted to resuscitate her but found that there was a hole in her throat. The paramedics covered the hole but unfortunately she died at the scene.

Two facts about this case ended up resulting in a huge amount of press coverage. The first aspect of the case was, of course, that Anna was white and from a respectable family. This alone would have been enough for the media to run with, but the second aspect of her victim profile ended up pushing this case beyond the realm of local news coverage and began bringing it national attention.

This aspect of her victim profile was that, at the time of her death, Anna Palmer had only been ten years old. There is hardly any crime out there that is more heinous than the murder of a child, but if the child in question has the racial and social profile that Anna Palmer did, the media will call it a national tragedy. The final nail in the coffin was just how well loved Anna had been in her neighbourhood, with her neighbours stating what a huge loss it was and how there seemed to be a hole in the community because of her absence.

And so Anna Palmer's case became the talk of the town, and law enforcement officials scrambled to get a hold of as much evidence as possible. A swift conclusion was necessary, else the Salt Lake City Police Department would end up losing face and being embarrassed by the media. However, this put the local police department in a real fix because they did not have much to work with at all. After a postmortem examination, forensic scientists ascertained that Anna had been stabbed to death and sexually abused prior to her death.

Also ascertained from the postmortem examination were some hints regarding the psychological profile of the murderer. The stab wounds were erratic and jagged. One of the stab wounds even severed the victim's spinal cord. This told law enforcement officials that the perpetrator of this crime was mentally unstable, probably had a history of violence, and that the thought process behind the murder was a combination of pedophilic tendencies and feelings of sexual inadequacy stemming from possible impotence. They also ascertained from the messy and uncertain nature of the stab wounds that this was either the perpetrator's very first kill or one of the very first.

Apart from this, however, law enforcement officials were hard pressed to find anything tangible to go on. This psychological profile of the suspect was only useful if they had a suspect to analyze and compare with. It was similar to having DNA evidence but no sample from a suspect with which they could compare it.

One particularly frustrating facet of this case was that, despite the fact that the murder had occurred near a busy intersection, there was absolutely no one willing to come forward as a witness. The reason behind this was unclear; law enforcement officials did not know whether this was due to the fact that no one had seen anything or no one was willing to say anything, so they offered a reward of eleven thousand dollars to anyone with pertinent information regarding the case. This resulted in a lot of calls being made to the local police department, a lot of potential leads being developed, but none of them turned out to provide anything tangible that would help solve this case. Mostly the calls consisted of people looking for easy money, people craving some sort of attention from a case so heavily promoted in the media, or people that meant well but did not provide any useful form of evidence.

In the end, law enforcement officials followed up on over a thousand leads in increasingly desperate attempts to get somewhere with this case, but none of them led them any closer to their killer. A significant amount of DNA evidence was also collected but, as is the case in most every cold case, technology was not advanced enough to allow them to match it to anyone.

To the dismay of the public, the case went cold, and ten years went by before anybody thought to reopen it. The violent nature of the crime made the victim stick around in the memory of Salt Lake City, but it was only after cases like those of Krystal Beslanowitch and Lucille Johnson were solved that law enforcement officials began looking into Anna Palmer's case again. When those other cold cases started getting solved, it gave the law enforcement officials originally assigned the case hope that the evidence they'd collected a decade ago would now be useful thanks to the advancements made in DNA analysis.

In order to gain fresh evidence, forensic scientists reopened the evidence kit made from the victim's clothing and analyzed it once more. A smattering of DNA evidence was discovered, but most of it was from the victim's own blood. This threw a wrench into the case for a little while, until the law enforcement officials that had been assigned the case realized that they could take evidence from a different source.

Thinking back to the nature of the case, law enforcement officials realized that the victim had put up a fight. A re-examination of crime scene photos and pictures of the victim showed that she had bloody nails. Law enforcement officials deduced from this that the victim had probably used her nails to scratch her assailant in an attempt to fend him off. This meant that there was a good chance that they could find the DNA of the murderer in the cotton swabs containing DNA from under her fingernails.

It is important to note the innovativeness of the forensic scientists at the time the victim's body was being analyzed. Examining a victim's fingernails was a technique not all that common at the time. This displayed out-of-the-box thinking on the part of the forensic scientists, something not often seen in a field that is notorious for by-the-book thinking. As we will discuss in a later chapter on the disadvantages of forensic science, such thinking is essential if the discipline is to progress beyond its stagnant current state.

Using several different methods for analyzing the DNA derived from her fingernails, forensic scientists, after months of hard work, were finally able to separate DNA that did not belong to Palmer. This DNA was from her murderer. In a refreshing turn of events, law enforcement officials did not have to wait very long for a hit, due to the fact that her murderer had continued acting on his pedophilic proclivities. As a result of his continued sexual attraction to children, and violence committed against said children, the victim's murderer, a man by the name of Matthew Breck, had already been arrested for a federal offence. This meant that his DNA could be found on CODIS, thus allowing law enforcement officials to get a hit in very little time.

Matthew Breck

Upon examining Breck, law enforcement officials realized that he fit the psychological profile of the killer that they had created a decade ago. He had been accused of a string of sexual assaults committed against children, finally being arrested for the sexual abuse of a child, sodomy, and lewdness of a minor only three years after he had murdered Anna Palmer. He had been sentenced to ten years in a federal penitentiary, eight of which had been served by the time law enforcement officials connected him to the murder of Anna Palmer.

After looking into Breck's personal history, they discovered that he had been living only a block away from Anna Palmer's residence at the time she was killed. He had been nineteen years old and the victim had almost certainly been his first kill. It was unknown whether he had killed any other children after Palmer, but the connection between him and her murder in 1999 was clear.

In order to build an airtight case, the prosecutor from the District Attorney's office who was assigned this case told law enforcement officials to obtain a fresh DNA sample from Breck and compare it to the DNA found under the victim's fingernails. Not wanting to leave anything to chance, law enforcement officials complied.

After obtaining DNA via a buccal swab, forensic analysts compared the sample with the DNA found in the skin cells that had been under the victim's nails. The result was a match.

It took the entire span of her life after her

death for it to happen, but Anna Palmer's murderer was finally apprehended. Had it not been for DNA analysis connecting him to this case, Breck would have been released in two years and no one would have been able to stop him from harming another child. Now that he has been connected to Anna Palmer's murder, he will spend the rest of his natural life in a federal penitentiary. The victim's mother, the neighbours that loved her so much, and all those who followed the case for so long, were finally able to breathe a sigh of relief.

The general consensus of everyone involved in this case is that the sole reason it was solved was forensic science. Truly, practically every other form of traditional police work failed; it was only DNA analysis that allowed the law enforcement officials assigned this case to finally make a breakthrough and put the decade-old murder of an innocent ten-year-old girl behind them for good.

Leanne Tiernan and Yvonne Fitt

The case of Leanne Tiernan[liv] is perhaps the most unique out of any of the cases in this book. For one, it is the case that received the most press coverage out of any other. Secondly, Tiernan's case did not remain cold for nearly as long as some of the other cases described in this book, as the trail only went cold for about a year. And finally, Tiernan's case was initially that of a missing person, and the new evidence that led to the reopening of her case file was the discovery of her body in the woods.

Tiernan, an A-Levels student living in Leeds with her parents, was sixteen years old when she was abducted. Her friend had last seen her when they parted ways while walking home from a shopping trip at the

Leeds City Center on November 26, 2000. Upon returning home, this friend phoned Tiernan's home to check if her friend had gotten home yet. She was surprised to learn that she had yet to get home. About twenty minutes after Tiernan's friend called, Tiernan's mother tried to contact her daughter on her mobile phone, only to have the call get cut off after a few rings. She tried again, only to achieve the same result.

Two hours later, Tiernan's mother phoned the local police department to report her daughter as a missing person. As is the case with missing person cases involving minors, the police immediately began a missing person inquiry. However, the general consensus among law enforcement officials is that if a child goes missing for more than three days, hope begins to dwindle of ever finding the child alive.

The chief investigator assigned to this case was a man by the name of Chris Gregg. To start off the investigation, Gregg organized police to canvass the area where Tiernan had last been seen. When no trace of her was found, the investigation escalated until it became the biggest inquiry into a missing person that West Yorkshire had ever seen, with over two hundred police officers and twice as many volunteers involved in the search.

When area canvass proved fruitless, Gregg began to go door to door asking people living nearby if they had seen or heard anything in an attempt to obtain a possible witness. A probable route for Tiernan's abductor was deduced and hundreds of tenants living in houses along this route were questioned, as well as those living in every single house within a three-mile radius of where Tiernan had last been seen. Despite the vigilance of the police department in this case and the efficiency in which information was being gathered, none of the techniques the police department applied were bearing any fruit. Even with their best efforts, the law enforcement officials that had been assigned this case were unable to find any concrete leads that would help them locate Tiernan. Out of the hundreds of people that were questioned, virtually none were able to provide any useful information whatsoever.

The investigation expanded, and every sex offender living within the Leeds city limits was questioned and interrogated. Supermarket chains printed Tiernan's picture on milk cartons, a ten-thousand-pound reward was offered for any information regarding her disappearance, all to little avail. The only headway law enforcement officials were able to make was obtained through the description of a man who had been seen walking his dog in the area Tiernan had last been seen. The description of this man turned out to be quite similar to the person that was eventually arrested for Tiernan's abduction and eventual murder.

Tiernan's phone had been turned off the day of her disappearance. Despite this, law enforcement officials attempted to contact her by sending text messages to her mobile number.

A witness soon came forward, claiming to have heard a high-pitched scream near the area where Tiernan had last been seen. People claimed to have seen Tiernan in towns and cities hundreds of miles away from Leeds. Eventually, with no witnesses, no concrete evidence and no leads to work on, in essence no trace whatsoever of the missing girl, the case went cold. Media attention died down, and the family began to come to terms with the fact that they were probably never going to see their little girl again, alive or dead.

Since there was no trace evidence to be found, even forensic science could not help investigators this time around. However, over a year after Tiernan had disappeared, when the memory of this enormous manhunt had started to fade from the minds of Leeds' citizens, all of this changed.

On August 20, 2001, a man walking his dogs along the road noticed something peculiar. When he went closer to investigate, he saw that it was the body of a young girl no older than sixteen. The police were called, and this is where forensic analysis finally started to give law enforcement officials the breakthrough that they so desperately needed.

Through fingerprint analysis, it was proved that it was the corpse of Leanne Tiernan. An odd coincidence was that her body was found no more than a hundred yards away from where the body of a prostitute by the name of Yvonne Fitt had been found buried almost a decade ago in the year 1992. This led authorities to suspect a connection between the two, but hard evidence of the connection would not be revealed until later on.

Although Tiernan's murder was incredibly sad, indeed it left the members of her family and the friend that had been the last person to speak to her in a state of shock, it was just what law enforcement officials needed. This was due to the fact that with her dead body came an enormous amount of something that would make it a lot easier for them to find out who did this to her: forensic evidence.

Tiernan's body had been wrapped very carefully in nine green-coloured bin bags. The bags had been secured using twine. Around her head was a black-coloured bin bag, which had been secured using a leather dog collar, upon which a quilt cover with floral pattern had been placed. Around her neck were plastic cable ties, which were determined to be the weapon that had been used to kill her via strangulation, along with a black-coloured scarf that covered up the cable tie. Similar cable ties had also been used to bind her hands and feet together. She was still wearing her hair in a ponytail that was secured with the same hair bands and clips that she'd been wearing on the day of her disappearance. Apart from these accessories, her body was absent any clothing, apart from her underwear, which looked as though it had been handled quite a bit.

Post mortem examination of Tiernan's body, as well as the way her body had been disposed of, told law enforcement officials a lot about her murderer. First and foremost, the fact that the black bin bag around her head had been secured using a dog collar lent much credence to the description of the man who had been walking his dogs around the same time Tiernan had been spotted in that area. Law enforcement officials now had a likely image of what their suspect looked like.

How much her body had decomposed along with the way it had decomposed indicated that she had been killed at least several months prior, but her body had been stored in a freezer. This could have been done for two possible reasons. First and foremost, the killer was trying to avoid detection. Secondly, he was trying to preserve her to keep her as a trophy, a reminder of sorts that would allow him to relive the crime whenever he wanted.

Law enforcement officials concluded that it was probably a combination of both. Cryobiology is a subdiscipline of forensic science, and it played an important role in analyzing exactly when Tiernan had been killed and how long she had been stored in a freezer, both of which were important details for the case.

Upon forensic analysis of Tiernan's body, forensic scientists concluded that she had not been sexually abused. However, the fact that she was not wearing any clothes as well as the odd position of her underwear seemed to indicate that there was a sexual motive to the crime.

Overall, all of the information they gleaned from the body allowed law enforcement officials to create a psychological profile of Tiernan's murderer. Judging from the way he had disposed of her body, law enforcement officials were able to deduce that, firstly, he was very experienced in the disposal of bodies, which meant that he had killed several times before and that he showed signs of obsessive compulsive disorder.

The lack of sexual abuse and rape but the presence of clear sexual motive seemed to indicate that the killer suffered from some kind of sexual dysfunction. He was either impotent or he received sexual pleasure from the act of violence itself.

With so much evidence to now work with, and forensic analysis on their side, law enforcement officials went to work trying to get to the bottom of this murder. The first piece of evidence that they worked on was the dog collar. Law enforcement officials contacted the manufacturer of the dog collar and discovered that they sold to over two hundred distributors. They contacted over a hundred distributors before they finally contacted one that gave them something concrete to work with. The information that this distributor provided was its sales records, stating that they had made sales to individuals in the Leeds area. Through these sales records, they were able to discover three people that had bought the same dog collar from the company that lived in Leeds. This narrowed down the list of suspects significantly.

On the forensic side of things, investigators began to analyze Tiernan's body for that all-important piece of trace evidence that would help them catch her murderer. The first piece of evidence that they analyzed was the scarf that had been around her neck. Upon close inspection of the scarf, forensic analysts were able to find a hair that had been caught in the knot. This hair was not blond as Tiernan's was, which meant that it belonged to her murderer. These forensic analysts extracted DNA from the root of the hair, conducted standard DNA analysis on it and began to develop the killer's DNA profile.

The second piece of evidence that these forensic scientists examined was the twine that had been used to fasten the garbage bags that Tiernan had been disposed of in. This twine turned out to be quite unique, as it was only manufactured by a company in Devon. This company usually only supplied its products to the Ministry of Defence, but they had on one occasion created a single batch that was made available for purchase to members of the public for the purpose of creating nets to catch rabbits in. The twine was matched to this single batch that had been made available to the public.

Once the origin of the twine had been ascertained, forensic scientists began analyzing the cable ties that had been used to kill Tiernan and bind her hands together. These cable ties were traced to a company based in Italy whose sole client was Royal Mail. This piece of information would become incredibly vital as the case progressed, especially when a final suspect was being named.

Forensic scientists were also able to obtain carpet fibres from Tiernan's body. These carpet fibres were also very unique because of the way they had been dyed. It was going to be easy to match these fibres to the carpet that they originated from.

Investigators also used a branch of forensic science called forensic palynology, which involves the analysis of pollen, to help build their case. Often considered by members of the public to be not very useful very often, forensic palynology's importance can be ascertained by the important role it played in this case. This is due to the fact that forensic analysts were able to find traces of pollen in Tiernan's nasal cavity as well as on her skin and in her hair. This not only told law enforcement officials that the killer was someone who lived near a garden, it also gave them another unique piece of evidence that they could match with their killer.

With all of this evidence and a list of only three people to look through, law enforcement officials found themselves in a considerably stronger position than they had a year ago when Tiernan had gone missing. Based on the information they had obtained from the forensic evidence, they were able to pinpoint John Taylor as the prime suspect in Leanne Tiernan's murder.

This deduction was based on the information derived from the evidence through forensic analysis. Taylor was an employee of Parcelforce, a subsidiary of Royal Mail. Hence, he was the only person on this list of three people that would have had access to the unique yellow-coloured cable ties, since Royal Mail and its subsidiaries received virtually every cable tie manufactured by the Italian company. This was enough for law enforcement officials to get a search warrant for Taylor's home.

Once they began to search his home, law enforcement officials were able to take advantage of all of the other information that their forensic analysts had been able to derive from Tiernan's body. First and foremost, the twine that had been used to tie up the garbage bags Tiernan had been disposed of in was discovered in Taylor's home. Additionally, the pieces of the same green plastic that the bin bags had been made of were discovered in Taylor's home as well.

The cable ties that had led to the search warrant were also discovered in Taylor's home. However, one forensic countermeasure that Taylor had tried to perform was to get rid of his carpets. Fortunately, this rather pitiful attempt by Taylor to throw law enforcement officials off his trail proved to be fruitless, as the forensic analysts were still able to find carpet fibres in the nails attached to the floorboards. These carpet fibres proved to be a perfect match to those found on Tiernan's body.

In a display of just how useful forensic palynology can be, forensic analysts were able to match the pollen in Taylor's garden to the pollen found on Tiernan's body. All in all, the evidence discovered during this search was more than enough to convict Taylor for the murder of Leanne Tiernan.

However, the prosecutors assigned to this case wanted it to be foolproof. Hence, they asked law enforcement officials to conduct a DNA test as well. Since forensic analysis of Tiernan's body had led to the obtaining of DNA from the hair found in the scarf, law enforcement officials were more than happy to oblige.

Taylor's DNA was acquired in the form of a buccal swab and compared to the DNA obtained from the root of the hair found in the scarf. After a relatively short period of analysis that lasted only a few days, a perfect match between Taylor's DNA and the DNA from the hair root was obtained. Hence, it was proven conclusively that Taylor was Leanne Tiernan's murderer.

In the face of such overwhelming evidence and Taylor's general lack of remorse and calm demeanour after the fact, the trial ended up barely lasting a day. Taylor pleaded guilty to both charges of kidnapping and murder. As a result, he was sentenced to life in prison.

Based on the fact that Tiernan's body was discovered so close to where the body of

Yvonne Fitt was discovered also sparked major interest. Fitt's case had gone cold due to a lack of evidence, but law enforcement officials speculated that Fitt might have been Taylor's first kill. Even though it was impossible to actually tie him to Fitt's murder, the coincidental disposal of Tiernan's body in the same area affected his sentencing. The manner in which he had disposed of Tiernan indicated that Taylor was well versed in the art of murder and the disposal of his victims' bodies.

The judge commented on the way Taylor had committed this crime, how the calculated manner in which he had stalked Tiernan and abducted her when she was at her most vulnerable proved that this was not a crime of opportunity or a crime of passion. This was the work of an experienced criminal.

Although Yvonne Fitt's murder still remains unresolved, the near certainty that it was Taylor who killed her has brought at least some sense of justice to the matter. Additionally, it has prompted law enforcement authorities to begin looking into Fitt's case and re-examining the evidence contained therein with the more advanced forensic technology now available to the criminal investigative process. If nothing else, Fitt's relatives and loved ones were, at the very least, able to take solace that the kind of man who would harm innocent girls will spend the rest of his life behind bars.

The importance of forensic science in this case is incalculable. Practically everything that law enforcement officials needed to locate and convict Taylor was obtained through forensic analysis of trace evidence. Even the oft-ignored forensic science of palynology came into play, showing just how the diverse fields of forensic science come together to help law enforcement officials of the world do their job more efficiently and more easily. This case is a prime example of just how important forensic science is in the criminal justice system.

Marianne Vaatstra

The case of Marianne Vaatstra[iv] is the second cold case in this book that pertains to a murder committed outside the U.S. It is also unique in a somewhat humorous way, as you will see by the time you finish this chapter, despite the fact that what happened to Marianne Vaatstra was not at all funny.

Sixteen-year-old Vaatstra was a native of the Netherlands and had been cycling home one day in August of 1982 when she was assaulted, sexually abused, raped, and murdered. Her killer slit her throat.

Marianne Vaatstra

Traces of semen were found at the crime scene, but forensic technology was not yet advanced enough for law enforcement officials to use it in an effective way.

Since the murder had occurred near a refuge for asylum seekers, and the Netherlands has a history of sorts with racial prejudice and violence against people of color, the blame fell on these migrants and it resulted in one of the largest incidents of mass racial violence in the history of the Netherlands. This violence against the migrants was based on the information that one of the Iraqi refugees had left the refuge center on the night that the murder had been committed and had not been seen since.

This Iraqi man was eventually tracked down in Istanbul, Turkey, by Interpol and brought back to the Netherlands. However, when his DNA was compared to the DNA derived from the semen found on Vaatstra's dead body, it was proven that he was not the murderer. Another asylum seeker of Afghani origin was also suspected but was similarly proven innocent of the crime after a DNA analysis.

The authorities decided that targeting the asylum seekers was unfair and decided to obtain DNA samples randomly from various men throughout the area. Almost two hundred DNA samples were taken, but none of them matched the semen found at the crime scene. A year later, law enforcement officials decided to create a psychological profile of the perpetrator, in which it was revealed that the true perpetrator of the crime would be a white male of Western European descent who lived within a fifteen-kilometre radius of the area, thus proving that the persecution of the asylum seekers had been grossly unjust.

Eventually, law enforcement officials ran out of leads to follow and the case went cold. Over the years, the case of Marianne Vaatstra became known as an example of the racial dynamics of the Netherlands, but at the same time, the fact that her killer was still out there became a reminder of the cost of poor police work. Seven years after Vaatstra's murder, politicians began to call for a reopening of the case and a re-examining of the DNA using modern techniques and technologies of forensic analysis.

After about five years of lobbying by various politicians, the cold case was finally reopened. The evidence was brought out once more and analyzed to see if forensic scientists had missed anything the first time round. In a shocking turn of events, the forensic scientists that had been assigned to the newly reopened cold case discovered that the DNA obtained from the semen found on Vaatstra's dead body was no longer accessible. Indeed, it had been disposed of when the forensic scientist heard that the case had run cold, presumably in order to make room for more DNA evidence.

This was an incalculable loss, as without this DNA that had been derived from the scene of the crime, the whole purpose of reopening the case to examine the evidence became moot. However, it is entirely to the credit of the forensic scientists that had been assigned to the reopened cold case that they did not despair, but found a solution to the problem at hand instead.

They got to work re-examining the evidence that was still available to them. Though there was not much DNA evidence still obtainable from Vaatstra's clothes, the forensic scientists were still able to find something useful: a lighter. This lighter had been found by law enforcement officials at the scene of the crime. Now that the forensic scientists had something new to work with, they immediately got to work and analyzed the lighter on the off chance that it had any DNA on it.

As it turned out, the lighter did have DNA on it, and lots of it. Just to be sure that it was not Vaatstra's own DNA, the forensic scientists conducted tests and compared the DNA to Vaatstra's own. The result was not a match, which meant that the DNA from the lighter almost certainly belonged to her rapist and murderer.

Although law enforcement officers now had DNA belonging to the perpetrator of this crime, they did not quite know what to do with it. Keep in mind that this was the Netherlands, not America. There was a centralized database of DNA but it was not nearly as advanced as CODIS. Still, law enforcement officials gave it a shot. The DNA did not find a single match from their database, which meant that Vaatstra's killer had not been convicted of any crimes before.

With no other leads to follow, and significant political pressure on them to crack this case and not let it go cold again, law enforcement officials were forced to get a little creative with their crime-solving methods. Hence, they initiated what would end up making this case seem very humorous. They contacted 8,000 men that lived within a fifteen-mile radius of where Vaatstra had been found and asked them, actually requested very politely, to submit their DNA for analysis.

Out of the thousands of DNA submissions they got, law enforcement officials were pleasantly surprised to find out that one of them matched the DNA found on the lighter that had been next to Vaatstra's dead body. Just to make this clear, the man that had killed Vaatstra actually submitted his own DNA to the police, practically giving himself up.

This man, whose name was Jasper S,[lvi] was soon arrested and taken to court. While on trial, he was called as a witness and asked to explain why he did what he did. Jasper stated that he was not a violent man and he had never harmed anyone in his life before that day. However, when he saw Marianne cycling home alone, something came over him. He approached her, threatened her with a knife and subsequently dragged her into the woods where he raped her. He then choked her to death with a piece of cloth and then slit her throat by sawing her neck with the knife thrice.

He claimed that the actual murder had stemmed from his panic. He did not want to be caught for raping a girl, so in his disoriented state, he decided that murdering her was his best option. According to him, he did not come forward himself because he did not want to abandon his family. He stated that he understood what he had done had been wrong, that he had killed an innocent girl and he had ruined the lives of her family members and loved ones, but the reason he hadn't come forward and confessed to his crimes was that he did not want to abandon his own family. He reasoned that he had seen one family destroyed, he did not want to see the same happen to his own family, stating that had he confessed at the time, his two children, who had been five and eight when he murdered Marianne, would have grown up with their father in jail.

Obviously unmoved by this rather pitiful attempt to paint himself in a positive light and earn some sympathy and perhaps a light sentence, the jury deemed Jasper guilty of the rape and murder of Marianne Vaatstra, and the judge was particularly harsh in his sentencing due to the fact that both the rape and murder had been committed in cold blood. The judge was also particularly harsh because Jasper had never come forward in thirteen years, yet he claimed to be a good man trying to do the right thing.

It is important to note the role of DNA analysis in this case. Not only was it able to help authorities convict a rapist and murderer, it was also important in exonerating two people that had been accused of a crime they did not commit purely on the basis of their race. The way the Iraqi and Afghani man had been accused harkened back to the Dark Ages, as well as pre-Civil War America, in the way people were accused based on irrational thought and a complete absence of logic. Indeed, had it not been for DNA analysis, either of these two men could have been wrongly convicted of rape and murder.

Jonathan Sellers and Charlie Keever

The story of Jonathan Sellers and Charlie Keever[lvii] is one of the more tragic cases in this book, as the victims were innocent children. Charlie and his friend Alton were two thirteen-year-old boys who decided, on Saturday, March 27, 1993, to take advantage of the good weather and go for a bike ride. At the last minute, the plan was changed and Alton decided not to go. His younger brother, Jonathan, decided that he would go in Alton's stead. Jonathan's twin sister wanted to come along, but Jonathan wanted it to be a boys-only trip, so their mother told his sister to sit this one out. Little did his siblings know: Jonathan had just saved both of his siblings' lives.

Charlie Keever and Jonathan Sellers

277

The boys were seen at a local fast food restaurant, then a local pet store, after which they were not seen alive again. When police were informed of the fact that the two boys had gone missing, they began to canvass the area but were unable to find them. Eventually, two days after the boys had gone missing, their bodies were found by a biker on the west bank of the Otay River in Palm City, California. The biker had first discovered their abandoned bikes. When he went to investigate, he smelled something rotten, which is what led him to the boys' bodies, just ten yards away.

The circumstances of the boys' bodies were hideous to say the least, with the state in which they were in showing just what a twisted person the man who had killed them had been. Charlie was lying face up on the ground, his head resting on a pile of his and Jonathan's clothes, his body naked. His genitals were bloody and looked as though they had been mutilated. More specifically, they looked as they had been bitten very aggressively.

Charlie's body was found underneath a castor tree. Jonathan, on the other hand, was found hanging by the neck from this castor tree. His hands and feet had been tied together and he was naked from the waist down. His genitals showed the same kind of mutilation and bite marks that Charlie's did.

Upon examining the crime scene, police deduced that the two boys had been lured to this area by a makeshift fort that had been built there. It was unknown if the perpetrator of this heinous crime had set up the fort himself or had used it as an excuse to bring the boys to a secluded place where he could rape and murder them without fear of being caught.

Forensic analysis was conducted on the bodies of these two children, and the postmortem analysis revealed two important pieces of information. Both of these clues served to further intensify the general psychological profile of the suspect that pointed to the fact that he was a deranged psychopath with absolutely no remorse. The first piece of information was that DNA was present in Charlie's mouth that was not his own. This DNA was found in the form of seminal fluid. His rapist had ejaculated in his mouth. The second piece of information was, if possible, even more hideous. It was that the bite marks that Charlie had suffered on his genitalia had been made while he was still alive. This meant that his rapist had been biting and mutilating his genitals while Charlie was still conscious, presumably as a form of torture.

Despite the horrific nature of this case and the absolute best efforts of all authorities involved, the case eventually went cold. As was the case in virtually every cold case in this book, the forensic technology available at the time had simply not been advanced enough to allow law enforcement officials to find the man that had raped, tortured and murdered these two boys.

Several years passed by after the case went cold. Maria Keever, Charlie's mother, could not stand the grief of knowing her son was violated and murdered in such a vicious manner by a perpetrator who still walked free, so when the case went cold, she began to act in the capacity of a private investigator, attempting to gain enough evidence to force law enforcement officials to reopen the case and try to catch the murderer before he struck again.

In order to investigate the matter, Keever

dressed as a homeless person, purchased a gun to defend herself, and went out asking questions. However, her investigation had one major flaw: she was assuming that the man that had raped and murdered her child was homeless.

To their credit, the local police department took the grieving mother seriously. They acted on the leads she gave them and even arrested the man she claimed was the prime suspect. However, the man was proven to be innocent.

It was only eight years after the case had gone cold that it was reopened once again. In a surprising turn of events, the investigation did not drag on as cold cases often do. As soon as they were able, law enforcement officials had the perpetrator's DNA derived from the semen that had been found in Charlie's mouth. They were able to immediately match the DNA to a man by the name of Scott Erskine.

As it turned out, Erskine was already in prison for rape. Law enforcement officials quickly obtained a fresh sample of his DNA, matched it to the sample obtained from Charlie's mouth and the case went to court. With so much overwhelming evidence, the trial was swift. The jury judged him to be unanimously guilty, and also unanimously voted yes to the death penalty.

Erskine was executed for the rape, torture and murder of these two boys.

The Victims of the Boston Strangler

The Boston Strangler[lviii] is often considered to be one of the most notorious serial killers in American history. The murderer of thirteen women in the 1960s, the story of the Boston Strangler is very different from that of the other killers highlighted in this book, but it is also uniquely important to the history of forensic science. As far as cold cases go, the case of the Boston Strangler is singularly unique because it remained somewhat cold even *after* the perpetrator of these murders had been apprehended.

This was because the Boston Strangler's crimes, as well as his apprehension, all occurred during the 1960s when forensic science was still in a fairly nascent stage of development. Additionally, DNA analysis was still almost a quarter of a century away from being discovered in the first place, let alone becoming advanced enough to allow law enforcement officials to use it effectively to solve a murder. Finally, the FBI's fingerprint database was not developed enough to be of any real help to the law enforcement officials involved in this case.

In order to understand the importance this case would eventually contribute to the field of forensic science, it is also important to understand the details of this case, starting from the very beginning.

If you were to analyze the headlines of all major newspapers based in Boston published in the early sixties, you would see that most of them often shared a common headline. This was because the biggest news story of the decade was the Boston Strangler. The only other newsworthy item during this time was perhaps the Beatles; such was the sensationalism that was applied to newspaper reporting around this case.

Between the years of 1962 and 1964, thirteen women were killed with fairly similar modes of operation. Each of them was strangled, and in all of these cases, the murderer had been let into the women's places of residence with no sign of a struggle. This seemed to indicate that either all of the victims knew the killer and therefore let him into their homes or the killer dressed up as a handyman or plumber, or someone they felt they could trust.

The first of these thirteen victims was a woman by the name of Anna Slesers. Aged fifty-five at the time of her death, Slesers was found on June 14, 1962. Postmortem examination of her body showed she had been sexually assaulted with a blunt object prior to being strangled to death with a belt.

Two weeks after Slesers's murder, an eighty-five-year-old woman by the name of Mary Mullen was discovered dead in her apartment as well. Although Mullen died of a heart attack, it was later discovered that this heart attack was induced by the Boston Strangler when he tried to grab her.

Two days after Mullen's body was discovered, two more women were discovered dead on the same day in separate locations. The first of these two was Nina Nichols, sixty-eight years old, and the second was Helen Blake, who had been sixty-five. Both of these women had been sexually assaulted prior to their deaths and both were strangled to death with their own nylon stockings.

About three weeks after this double discovery of victims, the Boston Strangler killed his fourth victim. Named Ida Irga and aged seventy-five, this victim was found in her apartment on August 19, 1962, murdered and sexually abused in the same manner as the other three victims. Only two days later, a sixty-two-year-old woman by the name of Jane Sullivan was found in her home after having been assaulted and killed in the exact same way.

Although Mullen's death was considered unconnected at the time, the murders of Slesers, Nichols, Blake, Sullivan, and Irga were clearly the work of the same murderer. This was deduced by law enforcement officials noting the fact that they were all of a similar age, had been sexually assaulted prior to their murder, and had all been killed via strangulation with a foreign object. This use of a foreign object told law enforcement officials that the murderer thought of his victims as inferior to him and that the murders were motivated by nothing more than the desire to kill. Had they been strangled by hand, it would have told law enforcement officials that the murder was personal in nature, which would have drastically changed the nature of the investigation.

Following this flurry of murders committed within six weeks, the media descended on this case with enormous sensationalism and, once it became clear that all three murders were the result of a single serial killer, dubbed the killer "The Boston Strangler." However, the sudden media tension appeared to have spooked the killer because there was a relative lull in the case for a few months.

When the killer resurfaced a few months later, he appeared to have developed a different victim preference. Whereas his first batch of victims had been fairly old, the next batch of victims he began targeting were significantly younger.

On December 5, 1962, three months after the body of Ida Irga was found and the media coverage had died down somewhat, the Boston Strangler claimed his sixth official victim. Sophie Clark was twenty years old at the time of her death, over three decades younger than even the youngest of The Boston Strangler's victims so far. The only thing that connected her to the Boston Strangler was the manner in which she had been killed, which was identical to the way the previous five victims had been killed. A little over three weeks later, the seventh victim, Patricia Bisette, was found dead in her apartment. She was twenty-three years old at the time of her death.

The reignited media frenzy once again seemed to spook the killer who went through a lengthy refractory period once more. After the murder of Patricia Bisette, the Strangler's killings became more sporadic, occurring with one to three months in between, but it seemed as though he had two types of preferred victims: single women roughly either in their early twenties or their early sixties.

Mary Brown was found dead on March 6, 1963. This marked a change in the Strangler's modus operandi, as the victim had been raped before being killed, something the Strangler had never done before. In his previous murders, the killer seemed to prefer sexually violating his victims using blunt objects instead. Brown had also been beaten and stabbed prior to being strangled to death, another aspect of modus operandi that differed from the Strangler's previous victims.

Twenty-three-year-old Beverly Samans was the Strangler's next victim, but was not originally connected to this particular serial killer. This was due to the fact that she was not strangled at all, but was instead stabbed to death, a complete change in the Strangler's modus operandi. She was found dead two months after Mary Brown.

Nearly three months later, fifty-eight-year-old Evelyn Corbin was found dead in her apartment, having been raped and strangled. Twenty-three-year-old Joan Graff was next, with the Strangler reverting to his younger preference as well as his original modus operandi involving strangulation via nylon stocking, although the recent innovation of rape was still involved.

The Boston Strangler's final victim was also his youngest. It also displayed a complete reversal back to his original modus operandi, with the victim having been strangled to death by a nylon stocking after having been sexually assaulted by a blunt object. Her name was Mary Sullivan, and she was nineteen years old at the time of her death on January 4, 1964.

Law enforcement officials were desperate for a breakthrough in this case but were not able to get much evidence that they could use from the crime scenes. The breakthrough eventually came, but not in a way anyone would have expected.

In October, right after the murder of Evelyn Corbin, a woman was visited by a man who claimed to be a detective investigating the Boston Strangler case. This woman let the man into her home and was subsequently attacked by him, tied to her bed, and sexually assaulted. However, this man, who was obviously the Boston Strangler, did not kill her. Instead, he apologized and left.

The woman entered a Boston police station a few months later and described the man who had assaulted her. This description allowed law enforcement officials to suspect a man by the name of Albert DeSalvo, a man with a known history of violent crime and sexual abuse, as the prime suspect, but not in the Boston Strangler Case.

As the Strangler's murders had been going on, a series of seemingly unrelated rapes had also been occurring in the city. When DeSalvo's picture was published, several of the women that had been assaulted by this serial rapist pointed DeSalvo out to be the man that had assaulted them as well. Hence, DeSalvo was convicted of rape and sentenced to jail time. This is where his connection to the Boston Strangler case began to develop.

While he was serving time for his rape convictions, DeSalvo had a cellmate by the name of George Nassar. During their time together, DeSalvo confessed to Nassar that he was the one responsible for the Boston Strangler murders, providing details that proved his intimate knowledge of the killings. Hoping to trade this information for a reduced sentence, Nassar approached his attorney with the information. This attorney informed the police, who came to the federal penitentiary where DeSalvo was doing his time to question him.

DeSalvo cracked under pressure and confessed to all of the murders, informing police about Mary Mullen as well, the eighty-five-year-old that had a heart attack before he'd been able to assault her. Police made sure that he was the Boston Strangler by asking him to describe the crimes he had committed. DeSalvo proved that he possessed intimate knowledge about the crimes, details that were not released to the press. Despite certain inconsistencies in the stories that could be attributed to natural loss of memory, it was clear that DeSalvo was the Boston Strangler.

He was sentenced to life in prison, but managed to escape only a few months after being incarcerated. A full-scale manhunt ensued, and DeSalvo was caught in a single day, after which he was transferred to a maximum-security facility. Six years later, he was found stabbed to death by an unknown assailant.

Throughout the entire story of the Boston

Strangler, from the moment the victims were murdered, until the moment that DeSalvo was caught, to the day he was sentenced to life, forensic science does not appear once. It is important to note this, because due to the absence of forensic analysis, *DeSalvo's guilt was never conclusively proven.* Yes, because DNA analysis and other methods of forensic analysis had either not been invented or were not advanced enough at the time, DeSalvo's involvement in the Boston Strangler murders could never be proven without a doubt.

Doubts regarding DeSalvo's confession came up when law enforcement officers began to realize that the thirteen murders allegedly committed by a single murderer might not have been so at all. They might in fact have been the work of several different murderers. This theory is based on the fact that the victimology tended to differ greatly, as did modus operandi in two of the thirteen murders. A serial killer tends to follow a very strict methodology and victimology. This means that if a serial killer strangles a sixty-year-old woman to death, he will continue doing so unless he evolves. Since evolution is consistent, reverting back to older victim types and methods of killing is highly unlikely.

This confusion regarding DeSalvo's involvement in the Strangler murders was further compounded when all of his close friends and family claimed that he would never have been able to commit such terrible murders. A year after he was incarcerated, DeSalvo underwent psychological evaluation at Bridgewater State Hospital. The psychologist who evaluated him claimed that DeSalvo was not the Boston Strangler, but was instead a very clever liar with a compulsive need to be recognized. This doctor insisted that DeSalvo had confessed to the Strangler murders because he craved the attention, not because he had actually committed the murders.

Several FBI profilers later also stated that the Strangler murders involved so many different modi operandi and victim preferences that it could never fit a single person. Additionally, a former fellow inmate of DeSalvo came forward claiming that he had heard DeSalvo learning from another inmate how the murders could have occurred, presumably so that he could lie about having committed them more convincingly.

With so much confusion regarding DeSalvo's guilt or innocence, the only thing that could prove conclusively whether he was who he said he was or not was, of course, forensic science. In 2013, DNA analysis technology was advanced enough for a comparison to be done between DNA found on one of the victims and DeSalvo.

The victim in question was Mary Sullivan, the youngest victim of the Boston Strangler, and the one that followed the modus operandi of the vast majority of killings. DNA found on Sullivan's body in the form of seminal fluid had been kept fresh in a forensic evidence kit. Since DeSalvo was dead, a sample of DNA was obtained from his nephew instead. This DNA proved to be a 99.9 percent match to the DNA found on Sullivan's body. This proved that there was a basis for the extraction of DNA from DeSalvo's corpse, so a court order was issued that allowed law enforcement officials to exhume DeSalvo's body.

Once the exhumation was complete, DNA was extracted from DeSalvo's remains. This DNA was analyzed and compared to the DNA that was derived from the seminal fluid found on Mary Sullivan's body. The result was a perfect match, proving that DeSalvo was responsible for her murder.

This also proved that DeSalvo was almost certainly responsible for ten of the murders. These ten were those murders that followed the same modus operandi and victimology.

The importance of forensic science is particularly notable in this case, interestingly enough not because it was used, but because *it wasn't used*. The lack of forensic analysis resulted in major uncertainty surrounding the case, as there was nothing to conclusively prove that DeSalvo truly was the Boston Strangler until decades after his death. It was only when DNA analysis came into play that DeSalvo was conclusively proven to be the Boston Strangler beyond reasonable doubt.

Is Forensic Analysis Effective?

It is often taken for granted that forensic science is an effective part of the criminal justice system. This is due in part to the pervasiveness of forensic methodology in television programs that fit into the police procedural subgenre. People just assume that forensic techniques are the most useful in the world, that they are an inseparable part of the way law enforcement officials catch the perpetrators of all sorts of horrible crimes. However, it is always important to analyze concrete evidence. Hence, this next section is comprised of criminals that were apprehended through the use of forensic technique.

Ted Bundy

Possibly the most famous serial killer in history, Ted Bundy is certainly the most prolific. With over thirty murder convictions under his belt at the time of his execution, Bundy had become the most wanted man in America when it was discovered that he was the one committing the serial murders that had shocked the nation.

Ted Bundy was initially convicted of kidnapping and served two years. Following this stint in jail, Bundy was on trial for murder in Colorado when he slipped through the fingers of law enforcement officials and fled to Florida. In Florida he killed three more people in the same insidious manner he was famous for. This ended up being his downfall.

The reason Bundy managed to evade capture for so long, the reason he was only arrested for kidnapping and not murder in 1975, was that he was so good at manipulating forensic evidence, or rather not leaving behind any forensic evidence at all. Bundy was careful not to leave any semen or blood at his crime scenes, and since he always killed his victims in secluded places there were never any eyewitnesses that could testify that they had seen him.

Another reason that Bundy was so elusive was his unique face. He had a face that was virtually featureless, despite the fact that he was considered to be handsome by many women. Law enforcement officials were often unable to recognize him after he altered his features only slightly, such as by shaving his head, growing a beard, or even just putting on a pair of sunglasses and a cap.

This elusiveness made Bundy famous, but in the year 1978, when he was on the run in Florida, the year he committed his last three murders, he was finally apprehended. His capture and conviction is owed to a singularly brilliant method of forensic analysis which was made possible by Bundy's own twisted proclivities.

One of the three victims he had killed that year had a bite mark[lix] on her backside. This bite mark was compared with Bundy's teeth and a match was made. This proved that Bundy had killed the girl, and since the modus operandi of the murder was so specific, it proved that he had committed all of the other serial murders as well. Bundy was convicted of thirty murders and was executed.

Bruno Hauptmann

The case of Bruno Hauptmann begins with the kidnapping of the son of a rich man. Charles Lindbergh[ix] was a famous aviator, and when his son was kidnapped on the first of March in the year 1931 and a ransom of $50,000 demanded, he paid it immediately and without a fuss. However, when his son was not returned to him even after he had paid the amount, the authorities came into the mix.

The child's body was discovered in May of the same year very close to the family home. Since Charles Lindbergh was a very famous and influential man, law enforcement officials were very eager to find the man that had killed his son. They did so using forensic analysis.

Law enforcement officials found Bruno Hauptmann, the man who had committed this heinous crime, by tracing the circulation of the bills he had been sent. They tracked him down and found $14,000 of the money in his garage. Hauptmann claimed that the money was not his but a friend's, but forensic analysts were able to match his handwriting to the handwriting on the ransom note. This was enough to convict him, and the abductor and murderer of a child finally got what was coming to him, thanks entirely to forensic analysis.

Wayne Williams

The murder of a child is an act most heinous. It is a universally acknowledged truth that if anything allows law enforcement to capture those who would hurt children in a more efficient manner, then this entity has justified its presence in the criminal justice system. The effectiveness of forensic analysis in this area of law enforcement can be proven by examining the case of serial killer Wayne Williams.[lxi]

Between the years 1979 and 1981, almost twenty-nine individuals, most of them children, were found dumped in a river after being strangled to death. Police began keeping a close eye on the river in hopes of catching the murderer in the act of disposing of his next body and caught a big break one night. After hearing a splash, law enforcement officials converged on the source of the sound and found Wayne Williams driving away from the river. They arrested him immediately.

Although he was now in police custody, since no one had actually seen Williams dump the body into the river there was no proof that he was doing anything beyond driving away from the river. This is where forensic analysis came in.

Over time, while police were staking out the river, forensic scientists had been extracting large amounts of forensic trace evidence from the bodies of the victims. During their postmortem examinations, forensic scientists found trace evidence in the form of fibres of clothing and hair. Law enforcement officials matched these fibres to Williams's clothing and matched the hair to both him and his dog. This evidence was enough to prove that Williams had been the one committing these heinous acts and he was put behind bars for it.

Clifford Irving and Richard Suskind

In the case of these two con artists, the crime they committed was not quite as heinous as the murder of a child. However, they did try to lie their way into a large amount of money, and the forensic analysis conducted to prove their crime was singularly brilliant, which is what makes their case such a great example of the advantages of forensic science.

Irving and Suskind[lxii] came up with a plan to earn themselves a whole lot of money. They decided to trick a publishing company into believing that they were writing a biography of the billionaire Howard Hughes. Hughes was famously reclusive, so Irving and Suskind assumed that he would never publicly denounce their book as being a fraud.

Irving approached a publishing company, convinced the company that he had been hired by Hughes to write his biography and that Hughes had agreed to speak only to him and Suskind. In order to convince the publishing company, Irving forged letters that he claimed were from Hughes. The ruse worked and the publishing company ended up paying the two con artists over three quarters of a million dollars up front to secure the rights for the book.

However, when the book was announced, Howard Hughes called the publishing company to tell them that he had not hired anyone to write his biography. Since Hughes was a recluse, he was only willing to speak to the publishing company by phone. Hence, in order to prove his identity, forensic scientists analyzed his voice and matched it with samples of his voice derived from his rare public appearances.

As a result, Irving and Suskind were proven to be frauds. Irving ended up spending seventeen years in jail, and Suskind ended up serving five, all thanks to forensic analysis.

Richard Ramirez, aka the Night Stalker

In the year that passed between the summers of 1984 and 1985, a serial killer that was eventually dubbed the "Night Stalker" by the media terrorised the south of California. The Night Stalker's modus operandi involved breaking into his victims' houses and attacking them while they slept. He ended up killing thirteen people and assaulting several others in unsuccessful murder attempts.

Although police were eventually at a loss regarding who this Night Stalker could be, a major breakthrough in the case came in the form of a phone call from a concerned citizen who had noticed a suspicious vehicle driving through his neighbourhood a couple of nights in a row. The citizen had noted down the license plate of the vehicle and provided it to the police. Since the Night Stalker had previously targeted the neighbourhood that the vehicle had been spotted in, police looked into the matter and managed to track the vehicle down by canvassing the area.

They were successful in locating the vehicle, but it had been abandoned. Despite the fact that they were unable to find the serial killer using the vehicle's license plates, law enforcement officials did manage to obtain a fingerprint from the vehicle itself.

This is where forensic science came in to save the day. The fingerprint database[lxiii] had just been stored on a computer, which allowed law enforcement officials to use this database to find a match for the fingerprint. The fingerprint from the vehicle matched that of Richard Ramirez. Authorities responded to this successful match by providing Ramirez's picture to the media, which began showing it at every opportunity.

The prevalence of his picture on TV news allowed a citizen to spot him and inform the police. Ramirez was apprehended soon after and was sentenced to death.

George "Machine Gun" Kelly

Prohibition era was a time of staunch conservatism and vicious criminals. George Kelly[lxiv] was one of the latter. He was involved with a variety of criminal activities conducted for financial gain, from bootlegging to kidnapping to armed robbery. The major crime of his career was also the one that ended up causing his downfall.

This crime was the kidnapping of Charles Urschel, an oil tycoon based in Oklahoma City. Kelly and his partner in crime demanded $200,000 for Urschel's safe return, a sum that was paid within a few days. Urschel was returned a few days later without any major injuries but with a lot of information regarding his surroundings while he had been kidnapped. He gave all of the details he had shrewdly noticed to the police. Although Urschel had been blindfolded, this ended up allowing him to notice things that he might not have noticed if he had been able to see. These details included whether it was day or night, and thus the estimated time that he heard a plane flying over the place he was being held. He also deduced that the place where he had been held was a farmhouse due to the fact that he heard animals, and he was also able to determine the amount of time a thunderstorm had passed overhead. The most useful thing that Urschel managed to do, however, was place his fingerprints on as many items as he could.

Urschel's shrewdness during capture gave law enforcement officials more than enough information to deduce where he had been held during his capture. Once they arrived there, they found Urschel's fingerprints all over the place, which proved that it was where Kelly had been holding him. Kelly was found near the scene of the crime and apprehended. He was convicted of kidnapping and spent the rest of his life in jail.

Gary Ridgway, aka the Green River Killer

During the years 1982 and 1983, a rash of murders occurred near Seattle and Tacoma, Washington that all followed the same modus operandi. The murders slowed down after this one-year period, but continued to occur at a more sporadic rate throughout the '80s and '90s. The victims were mostly prostitutes, which meant that not much interest was taken at first, but the sheer quantity of people that were being killed, the end count being any-where between fifty and ninety people, forced authorities to take the matter seriously.

By the end of the year, when the murders were most frequent, authorities had been able to identify a man by the name of Gary Ridg-way[lxv] as a potential suspect due to his history of acquiring the services of prostitutes and act-ing extremely violent towards them. Although investigators had a lot of DNA from the bodies of the victims, they did not have the technolo-gy to compare the DNA to a sample of Ridg-way's so they were never able to support a conviction. However, at the turn of the century when a new dawn arrived, technology was finally advanced enough for police to compare the DNA evidence they had found to connect the man that had committed dozens of murders to his crimes. Upon re-examination of the evidence and a comparative analysis with Ridgway's DNA, it was proven that he was the Green River Killer. He was arrested and ended up confessing to an incredible forty-nine murders, although it is speculated that the actual number of people he killed was much higher. He is now serving forty-eight consecutive life sentences thanks to DNA analysis.

Dennis Rader, aka the BTK Killer

For about seventeen years between 1974 and 1991, the town of Wichita, Kansas was terrorized by a serial killer eventually dubbed the BTK killer. The serial killer's name was an acronym of his modus operandi, which involved binding his victims, torturing them, and subsequently killing them. The BTK killer[lxvi] eventually killed ten people over the seventeen years in which he was active, and law enforcement officials were never able to get anywhere with the case.

However, the killer's eventual capture was a direct result of his egotism. He was very hungry for attention and would often send notes to the media and the police department, taunting the investigators attached to his case, similar to Jack the Ripper. He went silent for about thirteen years until 2004 when he suddenly resurfaced.

This resurfacing involved sending a floppy disk to a local newspaper. Times had changed greatly since the BTK killer had last been active. While he was active, doing something like this would never allow authorities to trace it back to him. Now, on the other hand, technology had advanced to the point where computer forensics could track him quite easily.

Forensic scientists were able to analyze the data on the disk and trace it to its point of origin. This turned out to be the Christ Lutheran Church in Wichita. When law enforcement officials converged at the church, they were able to capture the offender, a man by the name of Dennis Rader.

Rader was a regular attendee of church services and was far from the fearsome killer everyone had expected him to be. Police eventually gathered enough evidence, thanks to the trophies he had kept from his kills. Eventually, Rader confessed to his crimes and was sentenced to nine consecutive life sentences.

Jeffrey MacDonald

The case of Jeffrey MacDonald[lxvii] is an important example of a killer trying to use his knowledge of forensic analysis to cast suspicion off himself after committing murder. A member of the Green Berets in the U.S. Army, MacDonald claimed he and his family were attacked in their own home in February of 1970. He told police four attackers had burst into their home in the middle of the night and killed his pregnant wife and two daughters. He was the sole survivor with only minor wounds, which obviously made him the prime suspect in the murders. Physical evidence at the scene of the crime even suggested that MacDonald was involved somehow in the murders, but it was not enough to be conclusive. Eventually, the Army dropped the investigation due to the fact that there was simply not enough evidence, although it is often believed that the reason for dismissing the case was because of the poor quality of the investigation.

After a few years, the case was brought to civilian court when a forensic scientist claimed to have proof that MacDonald was the killer. It is important to note that the evidence provided was not in the form of DNA, fingerprints, or any other form of trace evidence. Rather, it was through forensic analysis and the recreation of the crime scene.

The forensic scientist slowly began to show the holes in MacDonald's story. MacDonald claimed that he had fended off his attacker using his pyjama top, which had forty-eight holes in it. However, the holes were far too clean and neat to have been caused by a violent attack. If MacDonald had actually used his pyjama top to defend himself, it would have been torn to shreds.

The scientist stated that if the top had been folded a certain way, the holes would have been created by twenty-one stabs which was the exact amount of times MacDonald's wife had been stabbed. The cuts corresponded with the stab wounds on her body, which showed that MacDonald had placed his pyjama top on his wife and stabbed her through it. This crime scene reconstruction proved that MacDonald was guilty and he was sentenced to life in prison.

John Joubert

The city of Omaha, Nebraska woke up one morning in 1983 to see on the news that two children had been murdered. One of the boys had been tied up with a type of rope that law enforcement officials had never seen before.

Acting on a lead provided by a tip, law enforcement officials began to track a man that had been noticed skulking around several schools in the city. Investigators were eventually able to obtain the suspect's license plate number and found out that his name was John Joubert,[lxviii] a man who worked at the local Air Force base as a radar technician.

Joubert was apprehended and law enforcement officials were able to convince him to confess by showing him the rope. It was the uniqueness of the rope that forced him to confess, as a similar rope was found to be in the trunk of his car.

In order to further solidify the case, police began taking samples of Joubert's DNA. They compared the samples obtained from Joubert to trace evidence found at the scene of the crime and got a perfect match. Joubert was also connected to the murder of a third child a few months prior to the double murder.

Joubert was sentenced to death by electric chair. The solidification of his case depended solely on the DNA matching done by forensic scientists, thus showing once again just how useful forensic science is in the field of criminology.

At the same time, it is important to note that there have been situations where forensic science was actually used in a negative way. These problems with forensic methodology are important to note because they help create a more realistic view of forensic science. It is important that law enforcement officials don't get myopic about crime-solving techniques involving forensic methodology, because such myopia is what led to the following cases, where forensic science was used in a negative way either intentionally or unintentionally.

OJ Simpson

This is possibly the most famous case that is referred to by individuals against the inclusion of forensic analysis in law enforcement. OJ Simpson[lxix] is widely considered to be guilty of the murder of his wife, Nicole Brown Simpson, and her friend, Ronald Goldman. However, much controversy surrounds this case, especially when it comes to the way evidence was collected from the crime scene and later analyzed. The prosecution presented evidence in court indicating investigators located two matching bloody gloves—one at the murder scene, and the other on OJ's property. The defense tried to argue that evidence, claiming both gloves were likely found at the murder scene and investigators planted one of them at OJ's residence. This was never proven to be true.

Additionally, there were major problems with the blood samples that had been obtained from the crime scene. EDTA, a chemical that is used during the process of DNA analysis was found in blood taken from the crime scene. The defense tried to claim this was proof that the blood had been planted there after obtaining it from OJ—but even though the lab technician who drew his blood never accurately logged exactly how much blood he took, the defense couldn't quite prove that blood had actually gone missing.

The detective in charge of the murder case, Mark Furhman, invoked the Fifth Amendment on the stand during the trial, leading some to believe these accusations could in fact be true. Furhman was also accused of being a racist during this trial. However, what most people don't know is that EDTA can also be found naturally in human blood, and no tests were ever completed to differentiate where it actually came from. Most believe the EDTA likely came from contaminated lab instruments used to conduct the tests.

Despite the trial's outcome, many doubts still remain in this case. This was an important case that highlights how investigators could use forensic science in a negative way.

David Kofoed

David Kofoed[lxx] is not a criminal in the classic sense. Rather, he was a member of law enforcement that was particularly inept. The case of David Kofoed shows how ineptitude of law enforcement officials can be exacerbated when forensic science comes into play, due to the fact that forensic analysis requires great care, precision, and accuracy in all things.

Kofoed was in charge of collecting DNA evidence, but he wasn't very good at his job. The ineptitude with which he worked often resulted in him collecting contaminated DNA samples as well as often mistakenly planting evidence. Such poor conduct from a man in charge of such an important job is very serious when you consider the weight his findings possess in open court.

Kofoed's case is extremely important and must be continuously objectively analyzed. It is important to know just how much of an effect improper collection of forensic and trace evidence can have. The evidence he collected was responsible for people's lives, due to the fact that people were often wrongly set free or put behind bars. It is speculated that Kofoed intentionally planted DNA evidence at a crime scene, which he claimed was accidental. He was convicted of tampering with evidence and is currently serving time in jail.

Pros and Cons of Forensic Science

The advantages of using forensic science are all derived from the efficiency with which they allow law enforcement officials to solve crimes.[lxxi]

Pros

1. **Cyber analysis.** Forensic cyber analysis allows the prevention of cyber crime and the apprehension of cyber criminals. This is especially important when one considers the fact that cyber crime is one of the most serious crimes that can be committed in today's modern day and age due to the fact that the world is so interconnected through the internet. The use of email tracing, IP tracing, and several other techniques that comprise computer forensics have been integral to the apprehension of many cyber criminals that were responsible for major cyber crimes.

2. **Postmortem examinations.** One of the most commonly used forensic tech-

niques, postmortem examinations are essential in ascertaining certain details about corpses that have been discovered with no identification on them. Postmortem examinations can be used to ascertain the cause of death, the manner in which the victim was killed, as well as the victim's overall physiology, all of which are extremely useful in helping solve murder cases.

3. **Key in vehicular accidents.** Forensic analysis and techniques pertaining to its methodology are very useful in cases of vehicular accidents. Vehicular manslaughter would be very easy to get away with if forensic analysis was not involved in the investigative process, especially when there are no witnesses to tell law enforcement officials exactly what happened. Forensic analysis involves examining the marks the tires have made, calculating the speed of the vehicle based on these marks, examining the blood spatter of the victim, and so on. All of these techniques greatly help law enforcement officials get to the bottom of what happened in these cas-

es.

4. **Identifies impacts of alcohol.** The presence of alcohol in a person's body can change the way a jury looks at a case. However, proving a person is drunk cannot depend on the word of an officer claiming that there was the smell of alcohol on a person's breath. This is where forensic science comes in. Using forensic analysis can help police officers determine conclusively how much alcohol a person has in his or her system. This may seem like a complicated process, but all it involves is having the person suspected of being drunk blow into a breathalyser.

5. **Integral to anthropology.** Forensic methodology is integral in the scientific discipline of anthropology. Its diverse uses include helping anthropologists determine the relationships between different ethnic groups, allowing them to gain a fuller understanding of the origins of ethnicities. Forensic analysis has been particularly useful in India, where anthropologists determined the different

migratory tendencies of ancient civiliza-
tions that resulted in the melting pot of
different ethnicities in present-day India.

6. **Helpful to clinical medicine.** Forensic
methodology can also be applied to clinical medicine. This branch of forensic
science can be used in postmortem examination, but it can also be used in
identifying abuse, whether it is domestic
violence against women or abuse
against children. This can be done
through the clinical examination of
wounds that the victims of such violence
have suffered. Forensic clinical medicine can also be used to ascertain
whether or not a victim of poisoning had
attempted to commit suicide.

7. **Integral to human identification.** Bio-
metric technology is a direct result of forensic methodology. The innovation of
fingerprinting has helped streamline
identification in a big way, allowing the
criminal justice systems of countries
around the world to develop extensive
databases of fingerprints they can use
to compare fingerprints found at crime

scenes. The result is an efficient way to identify perpetrators of crimes that simply requires the individual to have left a fingerprint at the scene of said crime, something that is inevitable in most scenarios.

8. **Vocal recognition.** Another advantage of using forensic techniques can be seen in the use of forensic phonetics. This can be used to identify the perpetrators of crimes in situations where their voices have been captured. The various techniques that are used in forensic phonetics are speech enhancement, in which audio files containing the perpetrator's voice is present but in a low quality, and tape authentication.

9. **Efficiently aids in criminal investigations.** The various important uses for forensic analysis include investigation into arson, forgery, fraud, lie detection and the like, all of which require forensic technology and analysis to solve in an efficient and accurate manner.

The major disadvantages that those individuals against the use of forensic methodology often speak of pertain to issues that are ethical, legal and financial.

Cons

1. **Cost.** A severe issue concerning the use of forensic methodology is that it is so expensive. DNA analysis alone often ends up costing thousands of dollars, and the cost of converting the entire fingerprint database onto a computer was exorbitant to say the least. This is due to the fact that the equipment that must be used in many methods of forensic analysis is incredibly expensive. Although costs have gone down in recent years, modern science still has not advanced far enough to allow forensic analysis techniques to be performed in a manner that is cost effective.

2. **Labour-intensive and timely.** Apart from being expensive in the context of money, forensic analysis also costs a lot of time. DNA analysis in particular can often take weeks to perform accurately, especially if the DNA sample obtained

from a crime scene is corrupted in some way. This is due to the fact that the whole process of DNA analysis involves so many subtle and careful techniques that rushing the process even slightly could cause a botched result, which could prove to be disastrous in court. The reason this is such a huge disadvantage is that the amount of time such methods of forensic analysis take cause the verdict to be delayed, which increases the chances of a mistrial.

3. **Requires precision and accuracy.** The amount of time required to conduct successful forensic analysis stems from the fact that it is such a delicate procedure that requires a significant amount of precision and accuracy. This means that even a minor error that occurs during the process of analysis can result in a wrong result. Considering that someone's life often depends on the result, due to the fact that they might be convicted of a crime based on the outcome of the analysis, the risk of an erroneous result is often considered to be far too high.

4. **May infringe on human rights.** A major disadvantage of forensic analysis, and DNA analysis in particular, is that it often infringes on one's basic human rights. Analyzing one's DNA can give the forensic scientist access to a lot of information about that person's biology that said person might have wanted to keep a secret. Information such as the presence of hereditary diseases, genetic history, and thus lineage and ancestry are all types of information that most people would consider very personal. Hence, DNA is often considered to be unethical for this very reason.

5. **Accessibility.** Evidence that must be used in forensic analysis is not always readily accessible. This is due to the fact that a sample from a suspect is required to compare with the sample obtained from the crime scene. The inability to obtain such a sample can often cause delays in the process, thereby delaying the trial at court and increasing the chances of a mistrial. Such situations have often occurred where individuals guilty of a crime were able to go free

due to the fact that the DNA analysis took too much time.

6. **Susceptibility.** A major disadvantage associated with forensic analysis is that the evidence can often be tampered with. This has happened several times over the course of the history of forensic science, as has been mentioned in the previous chapter. The manipulation of evidence occurs so often because law enforcement officials want the verdict to go a certain way and the forensic evidence may not support the verdict they want declared. Hence, manipulation of evidence occurs at a very common rate in order to influence a verdict that is unrighteous.

7. **Analysis is subjective in nature.** Often touted to be the biggest problem with forensic analysis is that, although the results of the analysis remain the same, the interpretations of said results are based on subjective rather than objective analysis. This means that the interpretations of the results of, for example, DNA analysis conducted on trace evi-

dence found on the crime scene can differ from scientist to scientist. This can cause major problems in cases where forensic evidence is the main element in the prosecution's case, due to the fact that the defense can often get a forensic scientist to refute the claims of the scientist the prosecution calls to bear witness.

8. **Politics.** Politics is a presence in almost every element of human society, especially law enforcement. The right to police is a power unlike any other. This means that forensic science is not free from politics either. Political influence in forensic science is so great that it can often repress forensic evidence and sway the verdict. Financial factors are also at play in the world of forensic science, as forensic analysts and scientists can often be bribed to botch the results of their analysis in order to sway or alter the verdict.

9. **Lack of industry standards.** Another major problem with forensic science is that it is not based on any established

standards. Most analysis outside the realm of forensics checks its results with precedents. In the case of forensic analysis, the field is so new that the precedents are still currently being set. Hence, the analysis of forensic evidence must be based on extensive research and study and is thus highly subjective.

10. **Stagnant Innovation.** Related to the previous disadvantage, innovation in the field of forensic science has become mostly stagnant. This is due to the fact that the approach of forensic scientists has remained the same for the past century, despite great advancements and innovations in technology. Really the only great innovation in forensic science in recent times is the creation of DNA analysis, and even that is analyzed in the same century-old method. In order to grow, forensic science will have to move past the techniques of analysis established in a time so long before our own.

11. **Confidentiality.** A major problem with forensic analysis is that maintaining the

secrecy of the results of forensic analysis is often a very difficult endeavour. Due to the amount of time forensic analysis often takes, the discovery of the progress of a forensic test that is being conducted can become quite easy at times. This makes it difficult for prosecutors to build up their case, as the defense is sometimes able to prepare itself for the result of a method of analysis and refute the evidence that is about to be presented in court. This can cause major problems for law enforcement in situations where the basis for the prosecution's entire case rests on the results of forensic analysis.

However, it is widely believed that the advantages of using forensic analysis outweigh the disadvantages. The problems mentioned regarding forensic analysis are real problems, but it must also be noted that they are problems endemic to the whole law enforcement system and the criminal justice system in general. The removal of forensic science from law enforcement will only result in the same archaic system of justice that prevailed before civilized times. Forensic science may not be perfect, but the good it has done is tangible and real. Hence, it is clear to see that forensic science is, in fact, effective.

Glossary of Forensic Terminology

While not all of these terms were used in the book, you may find this compilation of forensic terminology useful.[lxxii]

Abrasion

An abrasion is a wound caused to the outer layer of the skin. It is considered a non-serious wound, as it only damages the outer layer of the skin, also known as the epidermis. An abrasion is considerably less serious than a laceration and usually little to no bleeding occurs. Mild abrasions are usually known as scrapes or grazes and they do not typically form any scars or leave any sort of marks. However, in case of a deeper abrasion, some scar tissue, usually of a temporary kind, can be expected.

Accelerant

An accelerant is any substance that causes a chemical reaction to work faster. It is also a term used, broadly at that, to define any substance that causes the 'acceleration' in order for fire to spread faster than it normally would.

These are terms that are usually used when investigating cases of arson. A forensic expert would distinguish between a fuel and an accelerant, as the two are not the same things and the terms are not interchangeable. In chemistry, an accelerant is anything that speeds up a chemical reaction or a process in order to arrive at a result faster.

ADH/ADD

Accumulated degree hours (ADH) or accumulated degree days (ADD) is the amount of time that determines how long a body has been in a state of decay. Sometimes a body is found in a state of decay that makes it difficult to determine how much time has passed since death. This is when forensic experts use various signs and symptoms of the stages of decay to determine how much time has passed since death. Weather and insect patterns are very important when performing ADH or ADD exercises, as different weather styles might make it difficult to determine the time of death. Indeed, in certain cold conditions, bodies can remain preserved for days or even months.

AFIS

Automated Fingerprint Identification System (AFIS) is a national criminal history system managed by the FBI. The system is very complex and houses the fingerprints, identification marks, biodata, and electronic images of thousands upon thousands of criminals. According to various estimates, there are almost 70 million subjects present in the criminal Masterfile.

Algor Mortis

Algor mortis is one of the processes of rigor mortis. It is the change in body temperature followed immediately following death. Generally, this decline in temperature begins immediately after death and continues on until the body reaches room temperature. However, external factors can sometimes have a significant effect on the cooling process. For example, if a body is in a hot desert, instead of cooling off, a body's temperature will rise until it is the temperature of the desert.

Antemortem

Antemortem means 'before death.' It is a Latin

term used to describe any events that took place before death. Sometimes scars, markings, or other wounds are found on the body. A forensic expert can tell if these were caused before or after death. This is usually determined by examining the body to see if the process of healing or the congealing of blood has begun on the wound. Sometimes a body might get damaged postmortem during handling or for other reasons. These wounds can be used as evidence, which is why it is important to correctly determine the timeframe in which the marks or wounds were inflicted.

Anthropology

Usually, anthropology is said to be the study of humanity or humans, past and present. However, in a forensic setting, it is a term used to describe the application of physical anthropology where studies are made on bodies to determine facts when the body is in various states of decomposition. Physical anthropology is usually used during criminal cases. A forensic anthropologist can assist investigations by determining the time and cause of death when the body is found to be in various states of decomposition, burned, mutilated, water logged, or is otherwise unrecognizable.

Anthropometry

Anthropometry is the scientific study of the measurements of a human individual. Forensic anthropometry means to study a human skeleton in a legal setting. This is important when a biological profile is needed. Though a skeleton may look like any other to a layman, anthropometists can determine many things from just the bones.

Arches

During fingerprint identification, arches are used to classify one sort of fingerprint from another. Usually, a fingerprint can consist of three different types of marks: arches, whorls, and loops. Arches make up 5 percent of the fingerprint patterns that are recorded.

ATF

This is the name given to the Federal Bureau of Alcohol, Tobacco, Firearms and Explosives (also known as BATFE). This is a subdivision of the United States Department of Justice. The responsibilities of this bureau include the regulation and prevention of unlawful use of alcohol, tobacco, firearms, and explosives. The bureau keeps track of everyone connected to the aforementioned products, including manufacturers and distributors, so as to prevent any unlawful and illegal acts such as the production and transportation of firearms, bomb creation, or other acts that could harm other people or their property. The bureau also investigates arson cases.

Autopsy

An autopsy is a postmortem surgical procedure performed to determine various facts about the deceased and his or her death. The procedure involves a thorough examination of the corpse to establish factors related to the death, as well as to determine whether any disease or injury played a part in the deceased's death.

Ballistics

Ballistics is the part of science that deals with launching, flight, behaviour, and effects of projectiles. Forensic ballistics involves the analyzing of ballistics and projectiles. The forensic purpose of ballistics involves determining the examination of ballistics information of firearms, tools, and tool mark examinations as well. Forensic ballistics helps determine if a tool was used to cause a particular injury or a particular mark during the commission of a criminal activity.

Blood Spatter

Blood spatter and blood spatter analysis is one of the several specialty branches of Forensic Sciences. The use of blood spatter analysis is not a new phenomenon; indeed, it has been in use for centuries. However, modern sciences and technologies have recently enhanced this type of analysis.

Caliber

When speaking in terms of firearms, caliber is the term used to determine the size of the barrel or the size of the projectile shot from a firearm. Sizes range from the smallest of ball bearings, to bullets shot from rifles, to even bigger firearms. This determination of calibers, or sizes, can help to determine which type of firearm was used to wound or kill someone.

Cause of Death

In law, medicine and science, the cause of death is the reason or list of reasons that result in a person's death. Sometimes, these reasons can be determined at the scene of the crime by observation of the body, but if that is not possible, an autopsy can also help to determine the cause of death. A medical certificate is a detailed document that clearly explains how death occurred.

CCTV

A closed-circuit television camera, or CCTV, is also known as video surveillance. This is a camera that is used to transmit a signal to a specific place on a limited set of monitors for observation. These cameras are used in various public and private places to monitor specific areas or locations.

Chain of Custody

The chain of custody is a documented list of all the people who have handled a piece of evidence during a trial's proceedings. This evidence can be in any form, including physical or electronic. This list is particularly important in criminal cases, as it can include people who handled the piece of evidence both before and after the crime took place.

CODIS

CODIS, the Combined DNA Index System, refers to the FBI's program of support of criminal justice DNA systems, as well as the software that is involved in the running of these databases.

Cold Case

A cold case is the term used in forensics and criminology that describes an unsolved case. A case may grow cold due to lack of evidence, lack of leads, or lack of suspects.

Comparison Microscope

A comparison microscope is a device used to examine two samples side-by-side at the same time. Through a comparison micro-scope, two pieces of evidence can be viewed together to identify if they share a connection.

Composite Drawing

A composite drawing is a sketch made by a special sketching expert in a law enforcement agency. This sketch is made with the help of descriptions made by the victim or an eyewit-ness. A sketch expert uses the eyewitness's descriptions to sketch the suspect's likeness. The process is made easier if more than one eyewitness is present. These sketches can then be wired to different law enforcement agencies throughout the country to issue alerts and offer rewards for information.

Contamination

This is a term used in forensic science refer-ring to the accidental or purposeful tampering of evidence by mixing it with outside trace el-ements. Sometimes, when rescue operatives or law enforcement individuals arrive at the scene of a crime, they accidentally ruin crucial and important evidence due to negligence. This is known as contamination. Contaminated evidence is usually unfit to be presented in court.

Contusion

When a person suffers a blow, a bruise forms; if the bruise does not break the surface of the skin, it is known as a contusion. Contusions can be noted during autopsies, especially in cases when death occurred due to acts of violence. Contusions that occur prior to death can also denote if the victim was tortured.

Coroner

A coroner is an examiner of death appointed by a public office. Usually, a coroner is the person to alert law enforcement agencies when a death has occurred and if there is suspicion of foul play. A coroner is called in at death and it is his or her job to determine if the death was a natural occurrence, an accident, or homicide.

CPR

CPR is a first-aid method used as a life-saving exercise. CPR is short for cardio-pulmonary resuscitation and is one exercise that is taught during basic first aid lessons. This exercise can save a person's life in instances when the victim's heart has stopped or the victim is not breathing. CPR is a method that can help sustain life until rescue personnel arrives to treat the victim for whatever ailment they are facing.

Crime Scene Investigation Unit

A crime scene investigation unit is a team of specially trained individuals. These people are trained to gather even the tiniest bit of evidence from a crime scene without tampering with it or damaging it in any way at all. These individuals store evidence safely and transport it to the criminology laboratories where it is studied and analyzed as evidence to be later produced in a court of law.

DNA Blueprint

A DNA blueprint is storage of a biological profile of a person through their DNA. A DNA blueprint can determine such characteristics as a person's hair and eye color, making it easier for law enforcement to track down suspects.

DNA Profiling

This is a process where a person's DNA is used to determine his or her parentage and even include or exclude suspects in the process of screening for criminals. DNA evidence such as saliva, tears, blood, and sexual fluids can be found at the scene of the crime and then these can be used to create a DNA profile. Similarly, this profile can be used to convict or help acquit a possible suspect in criminal proceedings of any kind.

DOA

DOA is a term that means Dead on Arrival. This is a term used in forensic sciences to declare a person dead before they reached a medical facility. Sometimes, a victim might survive the initial attack but die on the way to a medical facility or in an ambulance. The factors determining the death are usually pulse, heartbeat, brain activity, and body temperature.

Entomology

Entomology is the study of insects. Forensic entomology is the study of insects to determine their relation to a crime scene. Deceased individuals are often found in various states of decay. An entomologist can help determine the stage of the life cycle in which insects (usually maggot larvae) are when extracted from a body in the state of decomposition. This can help to determine how long ago the death occurred or when the insects began to infest the body.

Evidence

Anything that proves a connection between a crime and the criminal is known as evidence. This includes substances that have been used, left behind, altered, contaminated, taken away, or otherwise left a mark on the scene of the crime.

Expert Testimony

Sometimes, an expert's advice is sought while viewing evidence. In court, experts may relay their findings and observations and conclusions, serving as a witness for the prosecution or the defense. Their professional opinion often sheds new light on the case. This testimony is known as the expert's testimony or analysis, and it helps the investigators solve a case.

Expert Witness

An expert who looks over the proceedings of a case and is expected to testify in court is known as an expert witness. An expert witness records his or her recordings and observations and draws conclusions from the evidence that has been provided.

Fingerprint

A mark left by the fingers on any surface is known as a fingerprint. Human fingers have special, minute ridges etched onto them. When a person's fingers come into contact with a surface, these ridges leave small, sometimes invisible marks on the surface. A forensics expert can help lift these fingerprints off the surface and later analyze them.

FISH

Maintained by the U.S. Secret Service Forensic Laboratory, the Forensic Information System for Handwriting (or FISH) is an electronic database containing handwriting samples from tens of thousands of writers. Sometimes, handwriting can help to convict someone of a crime. Threatening letters, confessions, or any documents linking a person to a crime can be analyzed through handwriting and linked to potential suspects by obtaining and comparing handwriting samples.

Forensic Science

Forensic science is the branch of science that is most closely related to criminal and civil law proceedings. This branch of science uses observational skills to determine evidence, collect it, and analyze it to determine the nature of a crime, and prosecute criminals. This is a very precise branch of science and has its own set of rules and methodology.

Fracture

This is the breaking, cracking or shattering that occurs in a bone. A fracture can occur when a bone comes in hard contact with any object. Depending on the contact, this bone can then shatter completely, break partially or only be damaged enough to form a minute crack known as a hairline fracture.

Gene

A gene is a unit of inheritance that is transferred from parent to child. This contains a person's DNA and can be used to determine a particular set of specific characteristics in a living organism.

Gunshot Residue

This is also known as cartridge discharge residue or firearm discharge residue. When a gun is fired, unburned primer powder escapes the gun and is left on the hands or the clothes of the shooter and, in cases where the target is at close range, can be left on the target as well.

Hemoglobin (Also Haemoglobin)

This is the iron-containing and iron-carrying metalloprotien in all red blood cells of all the vertebrates. Hemoglobin carries oxygen from the lungs to the rest of the body (i.e., the tissues). There, it releases the oxygen to allow aerobic respiration, which provides energy to the organism so that it can function and perform the process of metabolism.

IAFIS

The Integrated Automated Fingerprint Identification System is the national automated fingerprint search and identification system that is managed by the FBI. The system stores full criminal history and electronic images of the owners of the fingerprints it is home to. There are an estimated 70 million subjects in the Masterfile. The whole system can help identify a pre-recorded case in an estimated twenty-seven minutes, or even less.

Indented Writing

Indented writing is the writing that appears on the paper underneath the one being immediately written on. For example, when one writes on a notepad, an indentation of that text remains on the page or pages underneath the first page. This is known as indented writing.

Laceration

A laceration is a wound that happens quickly and tears through the skin so that the skin is opened and blood gushes out of it. A laceration usually cannot be healed by covering it with a bandage, in fact, stitches are usually needed to sew the skin together so that no more blood may escape and no foreign substance may enter the wound and infect it.

Latent Fingerprint

Sometimes fingerprints made by deposits of oil or perspiration on the skin can be deposited on surfaces. Latent fingerprints are usually invisible to the naked eye but are identifiable in the fingerprint databases. Latent fingerprints are made on non-porous surfaces, which makes it difficult for them to be lifted in the conventional and traditional methods of dusting. To lift latent fingerprints, forensic technicians often first photograph the print and then use a process called superglue fuming.

Latent Fingerprint Unit

A latent fingerprint unit is the group of specialized individuals who carefully search for and collect fingerprints at any given crime scene. This unit is specially trained and equipped to collect fingerprints from even the most difficult places. Latent fingerprint units are one of the most vital parts of a forensic team since sometimes even a partial fingerprint is enough to convict a criminal who might not have left a trace at the scene of the crime otherwise.

Ligature

A ligature is a cord or rope that is used to strangle someone. If a person has been killed by strangulation, a forensic team might search for ligature marks on his or her neck and throat area.

Livor Mortis

Livor mortis is the coloration that arises on a body after it has been dead and at rest in a particular position for a while. The cause of livor mortis is a lack of circulation. When a body has been dead for some while, the blood begins to settle. For example, if a person is laid on his or her back, gravity will cause the blood to settle in that area. This causes some discoloration in the skin where the parts of the body facing up will be paler and the parts of the body closest to the earth will be a dark red or purple color.

Locard's Exchange Principle

According to Locard's Exchange Principle, a criminal will always leave a piece of evidence at the scene of the crime, no matter how small. This piece of evidence will be treated as forensic evidence.

Loops

Loops are a type of fingerprint pattern. Fingerprints are formed by the tiny ridges etched into our skin as a result of DNA. A fingerprint consisting of the loop pattern has ridges that move in a circular pattern and double back into themselves. These move in a spiral motion and begin at the center of the thumb or finger and move in a more or less uniform spiral pattern outwards.

Luminol

Luminol is a powerful chemical that can detect the presence of blood even if it has been diluted up to ten thousand times. When investigators suspect blood has been removed or cleaned up from a given area, Luminol can be applied and the presence of blood, even removed, is detected easily.

Manner of Death

This is a legal declaration of the classification of how a person has died, made by the coroner. A coroner can declare a death as suicide, homicide, natural death, accidental death, etc. The manner of death is stated in the coroner's report.

Mass Spectrometry

This is a technique used by toxicologists to identify the chemical composition of a substance. A toxicologist enters the substance into an instrument that breaks the chemical down to the ions and then runs them through a series of tests. Different substances show up in different, unique ways on the spectrum that makes them easier to understand.

Medical Examiner

A medical examiner is an individual who has been trained as a medical professional but devotes all (or at least a majority of) his or her time to forensic work or assistance in forensic work.

mtDNA

The mtDNA or mitochondrial DNA is the type of DNA that is located in the mitochondrion of most cells. It is the cell that tells about the ancestry of a person. The mtDNA is passed down from the mother only and it is longer lasting than nuclear DNA, hence it can be extracted and analyzed even long after death and decomposition have taken place to determine race, ethnicity, etc.

Modus Operandi

A modus operandi can be anything that connects one homicide to another. Usually in a string of deaths caused by a serial killer, there is a signature style where the perpetrator uses the same type of weapon, attacks the same type of person, or maybe collects trophies from their victims. This is known as a modus operandi and it can prove to be a vital piece of evidence when the time comes to convict the killer.

Ninhydrin

This is a synthetic crystal compound that is used to detect amino acids. However, when used in forensic sciences, it is used to detect latent fingerprints present on the surface. It is applied to the suspected area and turns latent fingerprints purple so that they may be easily picked up and examined.

Nuclear DNA

Nuclear DNA is the unique set of DNA that is inherited from each parent separately. This is the unique DNA that is present in a person and is a mixture of both their parents.

Odontology

Sometimes the help of dentistry is needed to identify a victim. Odontology is the branch that helps identify a person through his or her unique dental records. Sometimes when a body has been mutilated beyond recognition, dental records are used to identify it. Similarly, if a piece of evidence with bite marks is found, it can be compared with a suspect's dental records to determine if it is a match.

Pathology

This is the scientific study of diseases, their causes, and their effects on the human body. A forensic pathologist can help to differentiate between the marks and effects a body may have suffered due to disease and the ones it suffered deliberately at someone else's hands.

Pattern Evidence

Sometimes, the evidence of a substance isn't as important as the pattern it which it is displayed. In a piece of pattern evidence, the substance of the evidence is less important than the pattern itself.

PCR

PCR or Polymerase chain reaction is a molecular photocopying technique. It can be used to copy and replicate DNA patterns for research and other purposes.

Perimortem

Perimortem indicates something that occurred at or around the time of death. This can be a lot of things, such as wounds inflicted on the body, an event that occurred that was in some way connected to the deceased, or anything that might be connected to the crime at all.

Person of Interest

An individual suspected of having committed a crime of some sort is known as a person of interest. This individual might be sought out by police to testify in a case or might be suspected of being the perpetrator of the crime itself. However, this title does not mean that the person has been convicted of committing the crime in question. A person of interest may walk away free of charge in the future if not enough evidence can be compiled for a prosecution.

Photography Unit

This is a group of professionals who specialize in forensic photography. This means that they not only perform digital imaging but also infrared, ultraviolet, x-rays, and other sorts of photography that might help find clues regarding a crime.

Physical Evidence

This is a piece of evidence that is usually found at the scene of the crime. However, sometimes a weapon or any item that helps connect a crime to a victim or perpetrator can also be regarded as a piece of physical evidence.

Physical Science Unit

The physical science unit is the group of professionals that deals with the application of physics, chemistry, and geology to identify and compare a victim to a crime scene or compare different crime scenes looking for a connection. A physical science unit examines the physical aspects of the scenes such as glass, paint, dirt, soil, mineral analysis, trace evidence, and any other sort of evidence that might help to identify and connect one crime scene to another or give some clue about the killer or their victims.

PMI

PMI, or Post-Mortem Interval, means the time that begins after death.

Polygraphy Unit

When a person deliberately tries to lie, his or her bodily functions change. These changes can often be detected by a polygraphy unit, which specializes in detecting misinformation. A polygraphy unit is also known as a lie detector for the same reason.

Post-Mortem

Events that take place after death are known as postmortem. For example, if a body is discovered in some state of mutilation, an examiner might examine the wounds to determine if they were suffered after death or before. If the wounds are determined to be inflicted due to accident or any other reason, even deliberately, after death, they will be known as postmortem wounds.

Presumptive Tests

Like the name suggests, these tests are based on some presumptions in order to identify the presence of one or more substances in a piece of evidence. For example, a blood test run to see if a person is intoxicated would be a presumptive test as the test was given to confirm the presence of intoxicants inside a person's body at the given time.

Professional Witness

A professional who testifies or offers his or her insight on a case would be regarded as a professional witness.

Psychology

Psychology is the branch of science that examines the relationship between human behaviour and legal proceedings.

Questioned Documents

Any set of documents that have gone through examination due to being regarded as potential evidence are known as questioned documents. These include handwritten documents, typewritten documents, documents that have been burned or charred partially. Additionally, the paper and ink used on these documents is also analyzed along with erasures, modifications, obliterations, as well as samples of indented writing.

Reconstruction of a Crime

Sometimes, a crime is reconstructed or pieced together using evidence from the scene of the crime to determine exactly how the crime occurred. This is done so that the detectives and law enforcement individuals have some idea as to how the crime took place and can often help them catch the killer or find overlooked evidence.

Ridge Characteristics

Over the years, fingerprints change slightly. However, there are some points of the finger-prints that remain the same throughout a person's life. Ridge characteristics can include ridge endings, bifurcations, ridge enclosures, and other ridge details that help to identify and match one set of fingerprints to another set. Ridge characteristics must be common in order for two sets of fingerprints to match.

Rigor Mortis

Rigor mortis occurs in a deceased body thirty minutes after death and lasts for up to eighteen hours. In this state, the body stiffens and goes through a series of various chemical changes.

Serology

Serology is the study of serums and other bodily fluids. In medical science, it is the study and identification of various antibodies present in the body for various diagnostic purposes. Such antibodies are typically formed due to the presence of various alien substances in the body that might cause an infection, such as in the case of blood transfusions, or could even be the body's response to its own proteins as is the case in autoimmune diseases.

SNP

SNP, or Single Nucleotide Polymorphism, or Simple Nucleotide Polymorphism, is a sequential variation occurring in the DNA occurring commonly within ONE set of population. This helps to classify different types of biological species that might otherwise be completely similar. This can help in identifying a person's ethnicity.

Skeletalization

This is the process that occurs after death. It is the stage of decomposition where all soft tissue on the body dissolves due to natural causes and detaches itself from the bones so that all that is left behind is a skeleton.

SOCO

An officer that is present at the scene of the crime or who is in charge of the scene of the crime is known as a SOCO, or Scene of Crime Officer.

Spectrogram

A spectrogram is a machine that recognizes, analyzes, and then provides a physical, visual representation of the frequencies a sound follows. This can be a sound that is inaudible to the human ear or it can be a sound that can be easily heard. A spectrogram can sometimes be called a spectral waterfall, a voiceprint, or a voice-gram.

Staged Crime Scene

Sometimes, a perpetrator might leave a string of false clues at a crime scene. The purpose of this is to throw the police and law-enforcement agencies off his trail, to mislead the investigation, or to lead the investigations away from him. This is known as a staged crime scene.

Super Glue Fuming

Sometimes it is not possible to develop latent fingerprints from nonporous surfaces. This is when the technique of superglue fuming is used. Via this technique, fingerprints are covered in a type of glue that reacts with the oils present in the latent fingerprints. This makes them easier to lift, as the ridges are transferred onto the lifting surface.

Suspect

In the language of law-enforcement, a suspect is a person being accused of having committed a specific crime or a specific set of crimes. Sometimes, especially in the U.S. law enforcement agencies, the word suspect is interchanged with the word perpetrator. However, this is a misconception, as a perpetrator is a person who is actually KNOWN to have committed said crime whilst a suspect is just that, a person who is suspected to have committed the crime in question.

The Ten Sections of The American Society of Forensic Sciences

This is a list of the ten major departments that make up the American society or academy of forensic sciences. These include: criminalistics, engineering science, general, jurisprudence, odontology, pathology/biology, physical anthropology, psychiatric and behavioural science, questioned documents, and toxicology.

TOD Time of Death

This is the time when a person actually died. Note that the time of death might not be the same as the time of discovery of death. In a case where foul play is suspected as the cause of death, it becomes crucial to determine the time of death as well. This is so that suspects can be ruled out, given they have an adequate alibi as to where they were at the time the death occurred.

Toxicology

Toxicology is a branch of science stemming from biology, chemistry and medicine as well. This branch is concerned with the study of chemical substances and their adverse effects and reactions on the human body. It is also a study of the harmful effects of chemicals, biological and physical agents that are present in biological systems. Toxicologists also study the dosage of any substance and its effects on the human body. An example of this might be studying the dosage of any medicine that is suitable to be administered to a human before it starts becoming toxic and harmful and has dangerous effects.

Toxicology Unit

A toxicology unit is the unit of forensic specialists who are trained to identify the presence of a substance at the scene of a crime or in a person's body.

Trace Evidence

When two or more objects come in contact, trace evidence is left behind. This is material that is transferred from one object onto another when they come into contact. This can be a piece of fabric left on a rough surface or hair, blood, and skin left on a blunt object after both surfaces came into contact.

Trajectory

A trajectory is the pathway a moving object follows before it comes into contact with its target. The object in question might be anything such as a bullet, a missile, a ball, or a satellite as well. When the earth orbits around the sun or the moon orbits around the earth, both are following a set path known as their respective trajectory. A trajectory can also be defined as the position of a moving object at any given time.

Trauma

A trauma is an injury that is caused to a biological organism, either living or dead, in some way. In medical science, a trauma is usually regarded as a physical wound upon the body by any outside and sometimes even an internal force. In psychology, a trauma may be a mental shock arising as the result of a physical trauma. A psychological trauma may also be the result of a severely distressing event.

Voice Print Analysis

Sometimes it is necessary to identify a person based solely on his or her voiceprint. This is when a voice is recorded and analyzed through a spectrograph. The spectrograph then provides a spectrogram where the voice is displayed in the form of a frequency with various ups and downs. This helps to identify the voice patterns between two sets of voices.

Voice Print Analysis Unit

A unit of forensic specialists who analyze voice prints, or personal identification that is produced by recording, analyzing, and then mapping out the sound patterns produced in a person's speech with the help of a spectrograph.

Whorls

There are about five different types of fingerprint patterns that are classified into different sets according to shapes. One of these is known as whorls. Whorls are ridges that move in a circular pattern similar to the flow of water in a whirlpool.

Witness of Fact

A witness of fact is the member of general public who testifies and gives evidence at a trial.

X-Ray

An X-ray is a form of electromagnetic radiation. X-rays are of shorter wavelengths than ultraviolet rays. These are used to scan objects from the inside without having to cut them open for examination.

About the Author

RJ Parker, P.Mgr., MCrim, is an award-winning and bestselling true crime author and co-owner with his daughters of RJ Parker Publishing, Inc. He has written eighteen true crime books, available in eBook, paperback and audiobook editions, which have sold in over 100 countries. He holds certifications in Serial Crime and Criminal Profiling.

Parker was born and raised in

Newfoundland and now resides in Ontario and Newfoundland, Canada. Parker started writing after becoming disabled with Anklyosing Spondylitis. He spent twenty-five years in various facets of Government and has two professional designations. In his spare time RJ enjoys playing the guitar, mandolin, piano, drums, steel guitar, and sax. Many years ago he filled in several times with the rock band April Wine, although Country music is his favourite.

To date, RJ has donated over 2,200 autographed books to allied troops serving overseas and to our wounded warriors recovering in Naval and Army hospitals all over the world. He also donates a percentage of his royalties to Victims of Violent Crimes.

If you are a police officer, firefighter, paramedic or serve in the military, active or retired, RJ gives his eBooks freely in appreciation for your service.

Contact Information

Email:

AuthorRJParker@gmail.com

Email:

Agent@RJParkerPublishing.com

Website:

http://m.RJPARKERPUBLISHING.com/

Twitter:

www.Twitter.com/AuthorRJParker

Facebook:

www.facebook.com/RJParkerPublishing

Author's Page:

rjpp.ca/RJ-PARKER-BOOKS

Crimes Canada: True Crimes That Shocked the Nation

By VronskyParker Publications, an imprint of RJ Parker Publishing, Inc.

An exciting 24-volume series collection, edited by crime historian Dr. Peter Vronsky and true crime author and publisher RJ Parker. Each month we will publish a book of some of Canada's most notorious shocking criminals, written by various authors, and published under VP Publications. Collect them all!

Robert Pickton: The Pig Farmer Killer (Volume 1)
By Chris Swinney

Robert Pickton inherited a pig farm worth a million dollars and used his wealth to lure skid row hookers to his farm where he confessed to murdering 49 female victims; dismembering and feeding their body parts to his pigs, which he supplied to Vancouver area restaurants and local neighbors.

Marc Lépine: The Montreal Massacre (Volume 2)
By RJ Parker

With extreme hatred in his heart against feminism, an act that feminists would label 'gynocide,' a heavily armed Marc Lépine entered the University École Polytechnique de Montreal, and after allowing the male students to leave, systematically murdered 14 female students.

But what motivated Lépine to carry out this heinous crime? Mass murderer, madman, cold-blooded killer, misogynist, political zealot? Or was he simply another desperate person frustrated with his powerless status in this world?

(NOTE: The case of Lépine has been debated among the most prestigious criminologists in the country. This account entails some of the most controversial opinions of these experts to date. The views of said experts are NOT those of the author.)

Only one thing is known for sure - Lépine's actions on December 6, 1989 radically changed this country and why he did what he did is much more complex than we will ever know.

Paul Bernardo and Karla Homolka: The Ken and Barbie Killers (Volume 3)
By Peter Vronsky

Paul Bernardo and Karla Homolka were so perfectly iconic as a newlywed couple that they were dubbed "Ken and

Barbie". But their marriage had a dark side involving sex, death, and videotape. The 'perfect couple' first raped and murdered Karla's little sister and then kidnapped teenage schoolgirls whom they enslaved, raped, tortured and killed while gleefully recording themselves on video doing it. Vronsky will take you on the journey from the Scarborough Rapist (Bernardo) to Bordelais (Homolka's current last name) and her return to Canada in October 2014 from the island of Gaudeloupe, where she lived for several years with her husband and three children.

Shirley Turner: Doctor, Stalker, Murderer (Volume 4)
By Kelly Banaski

On November 6, 2001, Dr. Andrew Bagby was found dead in a parking lot for day use at Keystone State Park in Derry Township, Pennsylvania. He had been shot to death. There were five gunshot wounds as well as blunt force trauma to the back of the head. He had been shot in the face and chest, as well as the back of the head, back, and buttocks. He was left face down in the parking lot in his scrubs, next to his Toyota Corolla. He died there.

The bizarre murder case of Andrew Bagby entails far more than death, although it has that threefold. It also brought to light a woefully inept Canadian legal system and the frighteningly dark mental descent of a woman scorned.

While evidence was steadily mounting against her, Dr. Shirley Turner dropped everything, left her car, apartment and every worldly possession, and went back to Canada. By the time Pennsylvania had an open warrant on her, she was in St. John's, Newfoundland, Canada. There, she gave birth to Andrew's son, Zachary.

While in jail, she wrote to a judge. Against legal precedent, this judge wrote her back and gave her legal advice on how to proceed with her case. The United States presented evidence of her crimes and their investigation and findings thus far. It was overwhelming. Her lies were exposed, her gun casings matched, and witnesses placed her car next to his at the time of the murder.

What happened next is one of the strangest decisions in legal history.

Canadian Psycho: The True Story of Luka Magnotta (Volume 5)
By Cara Lee Carter

Murder, necrophilia, dismemberment and an international manhunt – while the case of Luka Magnotta reads like a work of fiction, it is in fact a true story of an individual with a long history of mental illness in a gruesome attempt to gain notoriety. The horrific murder and mutilation of 32-year-old Concordia student Lin Jun shocked and captivated the nation. From the time the body was discovered, to the capture of Magnotta, and through the ensuing two years it took for justice to be served, the country anxiously waited for the outcome of the trial in December of 2014. This book chronicles the journey that led Luka Magnotta to become known as the Canadian Psycho. **WITH PHOTOS (Warning: Crime scene photos included that some might find extremely disturbing).**

The Country Boy Killer: The True Story of Cody Legebokoff, Canada's Teenage Serial Killer (Volume 6)
By JT Hunter.

He was the friendly, baby-faced, Canadian boy next door. He came from a loving, caring, and well-respected family. Blessed with good looks and back-woods country charm, he was popular with his peers, and although an accident at birth left permanent nerve damage in one of his arms, he excelled in sports. A self-proclaimed "die hard" Calgary Flames fan, he played competitive junior hockey and competed on his school's snowboarding team. And he enjoyed the typical simple pleasures of a boy growing up in the country: camping, hunting, and fishing with family and friends. **But he also enjoyed brutally murdering women, and he would become one of the youngest serial killers in Canadian history.**

The Killer Handyman (Volume 7)
By C.L. Swinney

A harmless-looking man moved to Montreal looking for a new start and to get off drugs. Somewhere along the line, his urge to prey on unsuspecting women, something he'd done and kept a secret for twenty years, became too much to keep inside. William Fyfe, aka "The Killer Handyman," snapped, leaving at least nine women brutally beaten, murdered and sexual abused (post-mortem). If not for the diligent work of a criminal forensic specialist and her discovery of a single fingerprint, Fyfe may have continued to kill at will, keeping Montreal residents, particularly single middle-aged women, frightened and sequestered in their own homes.

Hell's Angels Biker Wars: The Rock Machine Massacres (Volume 8)
By RJ Parker

For eight years, two outlaw biker clubs fought to control street-level drug sales in Quebec, Canada. The notorious Hells Angels went up against local drug dealers, the Mafia, and a rival biker club, the Rock Machine. Bombings and bullets was no stranger in the streets and many unfortunate bystanders got caught in the crossfire. When the smoke cleared and dozens of outlaws arrested, over 150 people were dead.

This true crime book depicts the history of both clubs and the events known as the Quebec Biker War.

Till Death Do Us Part: A Collection of Newlywed Murder Cases

By JJ Slate

Released February 28, 2015

Studies have shown that marriages typically thrive the most in the months after the wedding, a period known as "the honeymoon period."

Not these marriages.

Spousal murder is never acceptable, but newlywed murder seems to be on a completely different level. It is unconscionable to think someone could stand in front of his family and friends, pledging to honor and cherish another person for the rest of his life, and then kill his spouse in cold blood just months, weeks, or even days later. It happens more than you'd think—and, contrary to popular belief, it's not always the husband who acts as the aggressor.

In her third true crime book, bestselling author JJ Slate examines more than twenty true stories of newlywed murders, delving into the past of the victims and aggressors, searching for answers to the question everyone is asking: How does this sort of thing happen? These shocking cases of betrayal and murder might just make you think differently about those five sacred words, "till death do us part."

Serial Killer Groupies

By RJ Parker

This book delves into the twisted psychology of women attracted to some of the most notorious monsters on the planet, giving true crime readers real insight into this phenomenon.

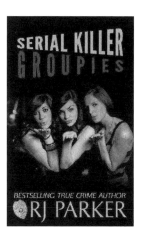

One of the most common reasons given by women who date serial killers is the fact that they 'see' the little boy that the horrible man once used to be, and they believe that they can nurture that kid, hence removing the cruel and harmful nature of the killers and making them amicable again.

Known as 'serial killer groupies' or even 'prison groupies' by some, a great number of these women have shown a surprising desire to get connected to the serial killer of their choice. Many of these women have become directly aligned with these killers, and some have even married these hardened criminals.

Groupies will do almost anything to get close to the prisoner they are attracted to. They give up jobs, family, spend money on him, and even move across country to be in the same town as him. Some SKGs are attracted to the celebrity status they acquire. They go on talk shows to announce their undying love for the serial killer and proclaim that he was not capable of these killings.

Missing Wives, Missing Lives
By JJ Slate
Released June 16, 2014

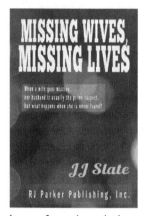

When a wife goes missing, her husband is often the prime suspect in her disappearance. But what happens when she is never found? In some of the cases profiled in this chilling book, their husbands were found guilty of murder, even without a body.

Missing Wives, Missing Lives focuses on thirty unique cases in which a missing wife has never been found and the undying efforts of her family as they continue the painful search to bring her home. The book covers decades old cases, such as Jeanette Zapata, who has been missing since 1976, to more recent and widely known cases, such as Stacy Peterson, who has been missing since 2007. Keeping these women's stories alive may be the key to solving the mystery and bringing them home to their family.

Social Media Monsters: Internet Killers

By JJ Slate and RJ Parker

Released September 18, 2014

In July of 2009, twenty-one-year-old Heather Snively logged onto Craigslist in search of used baby clothes and toys. She was eight months pregnant with her first child and so excited to marry her fiancé and start their family. She never imagined the woman she contacted on the site had plans to murder her in cold blood and rip the baby from her womb.

Who is really on the other end of that Facebook friend request, or behind that dating profile, or posting that item for sale on Craigslist? How can you be safe if you plan to meet up with a stranger you met online? What precautions should you take?

In this book, we've detailed more than thirty chilling true stories of killers that have used the internet to locate, stalk, lure, or exploit their victims. Facebook, Craigslist, MySpace, chat rooms, dating sites—it does not matter where you are online; killers are lurking in the shadows. They visit suicide chat rooms, search for escorts on Craigslist, and create fake social media profiles to fool and gain the trust of their victims. Someone you have been talking to for months, or even years, could be a completely different person from what you envisioned.

Serial Killers True Crime Anthology: Vol II 2015

By Katherine Ramsland, Sylvia Perrini, Kelly Banaski, Michael Newton, Peter Vronsky, and RJ Parker

Released December 15, 2014

In the 2nd annual *Serial Killers True Crime Anthology*, five acclaimed true crime authors present some of the worst, and recent, cases of serial homicide, including:

Joanna Dennehy
Enriqueta Marti
Douglas and Donna Perry
Brian Dugan
The Oakland County Child Killer
The Truck Stop Serial Killers
Rosemary West
Don Harvey
Michael Swango
Lonnie Franklin
Harold Shipman
Michael McCray
David Russell Williams

Serial Killers Abridged: An Encyclopedia of 100 Serial Killers

By RJ Parker
Released May 31, 2014

WARNING: There are dramatic crime scene photos in this book that some may find very disturbing

The ultimate reference for anyone compelled by the pathologies and twisted minds behind the most disturbing homicidal monsters. From A to Z, there are names you may not have heard of, but many of you are familiar with, including the notorious John Wayne Gacy, Jeffrey Dahmer, Ted Bundy, Gary Ridgway, Aileen Wuornos, and Dennis Rader, just to name a few. This reference book will make a great collection for true crime enthusiasts. Each story is in a Reader's Digest short format.

Parents Who Killed their Children: Filicide
By RJ Parker
Released April 30, 2014

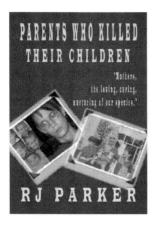

What could possibly incite parents to kill their own children?

This collection of "Filicidal Killers" provides a gripping overview of how things can go horribly wrong in once-loving families. *Parents Who Killed their Children* depicts ten of the most notorious and horrific cases of homicidal parental units out of control. Included are the stories of Andrea Yates, Diane Downs, Susan Smith, and Jeffrey MacDonald, who received a great deal of media attention. The author explores the reasons behind these murders; from addiction to postpartum psychosis, insanity to altruism.

Each story is detailed with background information on the parents, the murder scenes, trials, sentencing and aftermath.

Please feel free to check out more TRUE CRIME and
CRIME FICTION books and authors by our friends at

www.WILDBLUEPRESS.com

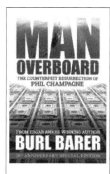

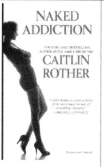

SIGN UP
FOR THE

NEWSLETTER

AND
UPCOMING
RELEASES

Endnote Sources

i   What is DNA?

ii   DNA: Promise and Peril
Linda L. McCabe (Author), Edward R.B. McCabe
(Author),Victor McKusick M.D. (Foreword) 356 pages
University of California Press; 1 edition (March 4 2008)

iii   http://www.dnapodcast.com/gregor-mendel/

iv   Why was Mendel's Work Ignored?
Elizabeth B. Gasking
Journal of the History of Ideas
Vol. 20, No. 1 (Jan., 1959), pp. 60-84

v   http://riaus.org.au/articles/a-brief-history-of-forensic-
science/

vi   The Forensic Casebook: The Science of Crime Scene
Investigation
Ballantine Books; 1 edition (August 2002) ISBN-13:
978-0345452030 332 pages
by Ngaire E. Genge (Author)

vii   Schafer, Elizabeth D. (2008). "Ancient science and
forensics". In Ayn Embar-seddon, Allan D. Pass (eds.).
Forensic Science. Salem Press. p. 40. ISBN 978-1-58765-
423-7.

viii The Washing Away of Wrongs: Forensic Medicine in
Thirteenth-Century China
ISBN-13: 9780892648009 196 pages
Publisher: Center for Chinese Studies Publications
Publication date: 1/1/1981

ix   http://www.pureinsight.org/node/1517

x

http://criminologycareers.about.com/od/Criminology_Bas
ics/a/Early-History-of-Forensic-Science.htm

xi   http://www.historybytheyard.co.uk/pc_gutteridge.htm

xii   http://forensicsciencecentral.co.uk/history.shtml

xiii   http://www.apa.org/monitor/2009/01/assessment.aspx

xiv

      http://www.sciencemuseum.org.uk/broughttolife/people/alphonebertillon.aspx

xv   http://onin.com/fp/fphistory.html

xvi   http://galton.org/fingerprints/faulds.htm

xvii   http://galton.org/fingerprinter.html

xviii   http://www.obscurehistories.com/#!fingerprinting/c1xpq

xix   https://prezi.com/v2hbllppylmg/the-story-of-fingerprints/

xx   http://www.zoominfo.com/p/Joseph-Faurot/859828012

xxi   Serial Killers Case Files, RJ Parker 2014 ISBN-13: 978-1490443515   302 Pages

xxii   http://www.essex-family-history.co.uk/camps.htm

xxiii   http://www.nzedge.com/sydney-smith/

xxiv   http://sussle.org/t/Keith_Simpson_%28pathologist%29

xxv

      http://www2.le.ac.uk/departments/genetics/jeffreys/biography

xxvi   http://www.sherlockian-sherlock.com/dr-joseph-bell-the-real-sherlock-holmes.php

xxvii

      http://www.sciencemuseum.org.uk/broughttolife/people/alphonebertillon.aspx

xxviii   http://en.wikipedia.org/wiki/Wilfrid_Derome

xxix   http://www.encyclopedia.com/doc/1G2-3448300331.html

xxx   http://www.encyclopedia.com/doc/1G2-3448300334.html

xxxi   http://aboutforensics.co.uk/edmond-locard/

xxxii   http://www.encyclopedia.com/doc/1G2-3448300424.html

xxxiii   http://www.encyclopedia.com/doc/1G2-3448300481.html

xxxiv   http://www.leamingtonhistory.co.uk/?p=891

xxxv   http://augusteambroisetardieu.wikispot.org/

xxxvi   http://en.wikipedia.org/wiki/Paul_Uhlenhuth

xxxvii   http://genetics.thetech.org/original_news/news16

xxxviii

	https://www.lssu.edu/campuslife/documents/buccal_swab_qa_032306.pdf
xxxix	
	http://www.bio.davidson.edu/genomics/method/RFLP.html
xl	http://www.exploredna.co.uk/y-chromosome-analysis.html
xli	http://www.exploredna.co.uk/mitochondrial-dna-analysis.html
xlii	
	https://www.utexas.edu/courses/bio301d/Topics/DNA/text.html
xliii	https://prezi.com/6ybp_usism32/the-case-of-dr-john-schneeberger/
xliv	
	http://www.atitesting.com/ati_next_gen/skillsmodules/content/wound-care/equipment/drains.html
xlv	http://www.myforensicsciencedegree.com/25-surprising-facts-about-forensic-science/
xlvi	http://www.huffingtonpost.com/2013/09/21/joseph-simpson-cold-case-cigarette-dna_n_3967517.html
xlvii	http://www.m-vac.com/news/press-releases/m-vac-systems-DNA-collection-device-helps-solve-18-yr-old-beslanowitch-case
xlviii	http://www.examiner.com/article/cold-case-solved-with-legos-fingerprints-on-toy-blocks-solve-cold-case-murder
xlix	http://old.stpete.org/police/news/2013-releases/oct2013/10-10-13-arrest-in-cold-case-sara-wineski.pdf
l	http://www.spokesman.com/stories/2013/oct/31/police-and-sheriffs-detectives-solve-23-year-old-c/
li	
	http://www.denverda.org/DNA/DNA_Cold_Case_Project.htm

lii https://prezi.com/w9bakjgum5cy/cold-case-of-patricia-beard/

liii http://www.sorensonforensics.com/forensics-lab-forensic-dna-testing/dna-forensics-lab-news-forensic-lab-development/dna-solves-13-year-old-cold-case-murder-mystery

liv http://murderpedia.org/male.T/t/taylor-john.htm

lv http://www.defrostingcoldcases.com/no-longer-cold-the-1999-murder-of-marianne-vaatstra/

lvi http://www.defrostingcoldcases.com/jasper-s-to-stand-trial-for-the-1999-murder-of-marianne-vaatstra/

lvii http://murderpedia.org/male.E/e/erskine-scott-thomas.htm

lviii http://nij.gov/journals/273/pages/boston-strangler.aspx

lix https://prezi.com/0itpg36omaj2/how-forensics-solved-the-case-ted-bundy/

lx https://www.fbi.gov/about-us/lab/forensic-science-communications/fsc/oct2007/research

lxi http://coldcasecameron.com/wrongfully-accused/

lxii

 http://www.infoplease.com/biography/var/cliffordirving.html

lxiii http://murderpedia.org/male.R/r/ramirez-richard.htm

lxiv http://forensicpsych.umwblogs.org/fbi/

lxv https://www.microtracellc.com/from-the-green-river-forensic-evidence-and-the-prosecution-of-gary-ridgway/

lxvi

 https://precisioncomputerinvestigations.wordpress.com/2010/04/14/how-computer-forensics-solved-the-btk-killer-case/

lxvii http://www.themacdonaldcase.org/Case_Facts.html

lxviii https://prezi.com/juuryjjct6zs/john-joubert-forensics/

lxix

 http://www.policeone.com/investigations/articles/7267753-OJ-Simpson-case-taught-police-what-not-to-do-at-a-crime-scene/

lxx   Body of Proof. 2015 by John Ferak, publisher Wild Blue Press, 238 pages

lxxi   http://www.scientificamerican.com/article/dna-sampling-pros-cons-high-tech-dna-forensics/

lxxii   Forensic Science: An Introduction to Scientific and Investigative Technique by Stuart James, Publisher CRC Press, 778 pages

Made in the USA
Lexington, KY
28 September 2015